CHRISTIANITY AND WAR
AND OTHER ESSAYS AGAINST THE WARFARE STATE

Books by Laurence M. Vance

The Other Side of Calvinism
A Brief History of English Bible Translations
The Angel of the Lord
Archaic Words and the Authorized Version
A Practical Grammar of Basic Biblical Hebrew
Double Jeopardy: The NASB Update
Christianity and War and Other Essays Against the
    Warfare State
King James, His Bible, and Its Translators

CHRISTIANITY AND WAR
AND OTHER ESSAYS AGAINST THE WARFARE STATE

by

Laurence M. Vance

Vance Publications
Pensacola, FL

ISBN 0-9763448-0-7

Cover print: *The Triumph of Death* by Peter Bruegel (1525-1569)

Published and Distributed by: Vance Publications
P.O. Box 11781, Pensacola, FL 32524
Phone: 850-474-1626   Fax: 850-937-1970
E-mail: vancepub@vancepublications.com
Website: www.vancepublications.com
Order Line: 1-800-363-9604

Printed in the United States of America

To Lew Rockwell,
Implacable Foe of the Warfare State

TABLE OF CONTENTS

INTRODUCTION

These essays, although organized under four headings, have one underlying theme: opposition to the warfare state that robs us of our liberty, our money, and in some cases our life. Conservatives who decry the welfare state while supporting the warfare state are terribly inconsistent. The two are inseparable. Libertarians who are opposed to war on principle, but support the state's bogus "war on terrorism," even as they remain silent about the U.S. Global Empire, are likewise contradictory. Christians who condone the warfare state and its nebulous crusades against "evil" have been duped. There is nothing "Christian" about the state's aggressive militarism, its senseless wars, its interventions into the affairs of other countries, and its expanding empire.

These thirteen essays also have one thing in common—they were all published on the premier anti-state, anti-war, pro-market website, LewRockwell.com, during the period from October 29, 2003, to December 2, 2004. Ten of them were written exclusively for that website and have never appeared in print until now. LewRockwell.com is the brainchild of Lew Rockwell, the founder and president of the Ludwig von Mises Institute in Auburn, Ala., and a leading opponent of the central state, its wars, and its socialism.

Each essay is reprinted verbatim, with the exception of the correction of a few minor errors. It should be noted, however, that the original spelling, capitalization, and punctuation are followed in all quotations. Because they were published on the Internet, most of the essays originally contained numerous links to documentation and further information on the Web that the reader could click on if he desired. Because this feature is not possible in a printed format, the reader is encouraged to consult the online versions of each essay at LewRockwell.com, where, thanks to the wonders of technology, they are archived.

Although many of these essays reference contemporary events, the principles discussed in all of them are timeless: war, militarism, empire, interventionism, the warfare state, and the Christian attitude toward these things. With the exception of the trilogy of essays on the U.S. Global Empire in chapter 4, which were meant to be read chronologically, the essays can be read in any order.

The first chapter of the book, "Christianity and War," and especially the initial essay of the same name (which also furnishes the book with its title), should be regarded as the key portion of the book. War is a subject that needlessly divides and sidetracks Christians. It is the author's contention that Christian enthusiasm for the state, its wars, and its politicians is an affront to the Saviour, contrary to Scripture, and a demonstration of the profound ignorance many Christians have of history.

Chapter 2, "The Evils of War," explores the views of our Founding Fathers on war and standing armies. In chapter 3, "Specific Wars," the evils of war and the warfare state are examined through specific wars in three different centuries: the Crimean War (1854–1856), World War I (1914–1918), and the Iraq War (2003–). In chapter 4, "The U.S. Global Empire," the extent of the growing U.S. Empire of bases and troops is revealed and critiqued.

The books listed at the close under "For Further Reading" include not only some of the more important books referenced in the essays, but other recommended works that relate in some way to the warfare state. Most of them are available from Amazon.com. The inclusion of any book should not be taken as a blanket endorsement of everything contained in the book.

It is my desire in all of these essays to show, as Randolph Bourne said many years ago, that "war is the health of the state."

Christianity and War

CHRISTIANITY AND WAR

"We will export death and violence to the four corners of the earth in defense of our great nation." ~ The Bush Administration

"From whence come wars and fightings among you? Come they not hence, even of your lusts that war in your members?" ~ James 4:1

"War is the health of the state." ~ Randolph Bourne

"War is a racket. It always has been. It is possibly the oldest, easily the most profitable, surely the most vicious. It is the only one international in scope. It is the only one in which the profits are reckoned in dollars and the losses in lives." ~ U.S. Marine Corps Major General Smedley Butler

"War prosperity is like the prosperity that an earthquake or a plague brings. The earthquake means good business for construction workers, and cholera improves the business of physicians, pharmacists, and undertakers; but no one has for that reason yet sought to celebrate earthquakes and cholera as stimulators of the productive forces in the general interest." ~ Ludwig von Mises

"War is God's judgment on sin here; hell is God's judgment on sin hereafter." ~ Bob Jones Sr.

"I saw in the whole Christian world a license of fighting at which even barbarous nations might blush. Wars were begun on trifling pretexts or none at all, and carried on without any reference of law, Divine or human." ~ Hugo Grotius

"Our wars, for the most part, proceed either from ambition, from anger and malice, from the mere wantonness of unbridled power, or from some other mental distemper." ~ Desiderius Erasmus

That the ongoing undeclared "war" in Iraq is supported by apologists for what World War II general, and later president, Dwight Eisenhower, called the "military-industrial complex" is no surprise. What is surprising, however, is the present degree of Christian enthusiasm for war.

Our Christian forefathers thought differently, as will presently be seen.

"Just war theory," although it has been misused by political leaders to encourage soldiers to needlessly fight, kill, bleed, and die, with the full support of the civilian populace, including many of its Christians, is nevertheless still relevant in this age of tanks, bombs, land mines, and "weapons of mass destruction."

In his 1625 treatise *De Jure Belli Ac Pacis (On the Law of War and Peace)*, the famed Dutch Christian, Hugo Grotius (1538–1645), universally recognized as the "Father of International Law," set forth six *jus ad bellum* (just recourse to war) conditions that limit a nation's legitimate recourse to war: just cause (correct intention [self-defense] with an objective), proportionality (grave enough situation to warrant war), reasonable chance for success (obtainable objectives), public declaration (fair warning, opportunity for avoidance), declaration only by legitimate authority, and last resort (all other options eliminated).*

Or, as the historian and economist, Murray Rothbard (1926–1995), said, in making his case that America has only had two just wars (1776 & 1861), "A just war exists when a people tries to ward off the threat of coercive domination by another people, or to overthrow an already-existing domination. A war is unjust, on the other hand, when a people try to impose domination on another people, or try to retain an already existing coercive rule over them."

Grotius also articulated three *jus in bello* (justice in the course of war) conditions that govern just and fair conduct in war: legitimate targets (only combatants, not civilians), proportionality (means may not exceed what is warranted by the cause), and treatment of prisoners (combatants are through capture rendered noncombatants).*

*I am indebted for these paragraphs on Grotius to Laurie Calhoun, "Just War? Moral Soldiers?" *Independent Review*, IV, 3 (Winter 2000), pp. 325–345, and for Joe Stromberg of the Mises Institute for bringing her article to my attention.

Grotius' fellow Dutchman, Desiderius Erasmus (1466–1536), was certainly no pacifist, yet he lamented: "War would be understandable among the beasts, for they lack natural reason; it is an aberration among men because the evil of war can be easily understood through the use of reason alone. War, however, is inconceivable among Christians because it is not only rationally objectionable but, even more important, ethically inadmissible."

The fact that a government claims a war is just is irrelevant, for American history is replete with examples of American presidents who have exaggerated, misinformed, misrepresented, and lied to deceive the American people into supporting wars that they would not have supported if they had known the facts.

In 1846 President James Polk, after Texas' accession to the union, deliberately put U.S. troops into an area still complicated by the existence of a boundary dispute with Mexico so as to be able to go to Congress with an incident and get a declaration of war.

In 1861 President Abraham Lincoln waged war on his own people after declaring in his First Inaugural Address: "I have no purpose, directly or indirectly, to interfere with the institution of slavery in the States where it exists. I believe I have no lawful right to do so, and I have no inclination to do so."

In 1898 President William McKinley began a "splendid little war" with Spain over Cuba. Its sequel to secure U.S. colonial power in the Philippines left dead 4,000 U.S. troops, more than 20,000 Filipino fighters, and more than 220,000 Filipino civilians, all based on the news-media slogan "Remember the *Maine!*"

In 1916 President Woodrow Wilson sought reelection on the slogan "he kept us out of war," but then proceeded, soon after his second inauguration, to ask Congress for a declaration of war: "a war to end all wars" to "make the world safe for democracy."

In 1940 President Franklin Roosevelt campaigned for his third term, saying, "I have said this before, but I shall say it again and again: Your boys are not going to be sent into any foreign wars." It was not long, however, before our "boys" were back once again on European soil.

In 1964 President Lyndon Johnson announced to a crowd at Akron University: "We are not about to send American boys 9 or 10,000 miles away from home to do what Asian boys ought to be doing for themselves." This was followed by the 1964 Gulf of Tonkin Resolution that saw over 500,000 "American boys" fight an "Asian boys" war. Over 50,000 of them came home in body bags.

In 1991 President George Bush I used faked satellite photos to gain Saudi participation in the first Gulf War, and to convince the American people that Hussein must be stopped from conquering the whole region.

In 2003 President George Bush II insisted on the need to "end a brutal regime, whose aggression and weapons of mass destruction make it a unique threat to the world." The holes in this statement have been unfolding before our eyes.

Yet, the gullible Christian theologian Loraine Boettner (1901–1990), in his book *The Christian Attitude Toward War*, claims that the United States has "never had a militarist president." He even advocates that the government "should be given the benefit of the doubt" when it comes to waging war.

But contrary to Boettner, and as mentioned previously, our Christian forefathers, being much better read and having a much better grasp of history than the modern Christian who spends all his time in front of the Internet and the television, had no enthusiasm for war at all.

Back before the Civil War, when the Christians published theological journals worth reading, two Baptist ministers writing in *The Christian Review* demonstrated that Christian war fever was contrary to the New Testament.

Veritatis Amans, in his 1847 article "Can War, Under Any Circumstances, Be Justified on the Principles of the Christian Religion?" approached the subject from the standpoint of war being justified only in cases of self-defense. Another Baptist preacher, in an unsigned article from 1838 entitled "Wickedness of War," approached the subject from the standpoint of the nature of war in general. Both articles look to the New Testament as their authority.

Amans begins: "War has ever been the scourge of the human race. The history of the past is little else than a chronicle of deadly feuds, irreconcilable hate, and exterminating warfare. The extension of empire, the love of glory, and thirst for fame, have been more fatal to men than famine or pestilence, or the fiercest elements of nature."

"And what is more sad and painful, many of the wars whose desolating surges have deluged the earth, have been carried on in the name and under the sanction of those who profess the name of Christ."

"It has not been till recently, that the disciples of Christ have been conscious of the enormous wickedness of war as it usually exists. And even now there are many who do not frown upon it with that disapprobation and abhorrence, which an evil of such magnitude as an unjust war deserves."

"Wars of every kind may be included under two classes—offensive and defensive. Concerning the former we shall say nothing. We need not delay a moment to discuss a question so directly at variance with the dictates of conscience, and the principles of revealed religion."

"But under what circumstances is war truly defensive? We reply, when its object is to repel an invasion; when there is no alternative but to submit to bondage and death, or to resist."

The anonymous Baptist preacher writing in a 1838 issue of *The Christian Review* continues: "The war spirit is so wrought into the texture of governments, and the habits of national thinking, and even into our very festivals and pomps, that its occasional recurrence is deemed a matter of unavoidable necessity."

War "contradicts the genius and intention of Christianity," "sets at nought the example of Jesus," and "is inconsistent not only with the general structure and nature of Christianity and the example of Jesus, but it violates all the express precepts of the New Testament."

"Christianity requires us to seek to amend the condition of

man. But war cannot do this. The world is no better for all the wars of five thousand years. Christianity, if it prevailed, would make the earth a paradise. War, where it prevails, makes it a slaughter-house, a den of thieves, a brothel, a hell. Christianity cancels the laws of retaliation. War is based upon that very principle. Christianity is the remedy for all human woes. War produces every woe known to man."

"The causes of war, as well as war itself, are contrary to the gospel. It originates in the worst passions and the worst aims. We may always trace it to the thirst of revenge, the acquisition of territory, the monopoly of commerce, the quarrels of kings, the intrigues of ministers, the coercion of religious opinion, the acquisition of disputed crowns, or some other source, equally culpable; but never has any war, devised by man, been founded on holy tempers and Christian principles."

"It should be remembered, that in no case, even under the Old Testament, was war appointed to decide doubtful questions, or to settle quarrels, but to inflict national punishment. They were intended, as are pestilence and famine, to chastise nations guilty of provoking God. Such is never the pretext of modern war; and if it were, it would require divine authority, which, as has just been said, would induce even members of the Peace Society to fight."

The "criminality of war," as Howard Malcom, president of Georgetown College, wrote in 1845, is not "that tyrants should lead men into wars of pride and conquest," but that "the people, in governments comparatively free, should so readily lend themselves to a business in which they bear all the sufferings, can gain nothing, and may lose all." That people would act this way, Malcom says, is an "astonishment indeed." "But," he continues, "the chief wonder is that Christians, followers of the Prince of Peace, should have concurred in this mad idolatry of strife, and thus been inconsistent not only with themselves, but with the very genius of their system."

The Founding Fathers of this country, many of whom were deists, had more sense than many twenty-first-century Christians when it came to espousing a policy of peace through nonintervention; in other words, not being "a busybody in other men's matters" (1 Peter 4:15). George Washington: "The great rule of conduct for us in regard to foreign nations is, in extending our commercial relations to have with them as little political connection as possible." Thomas Jefferson: "Peace, commerce, and honest friendship with all nations—entangling alliances with none." John Quincy Adams: "America . . . goes not abroad seeking monsters to destroy."

So the War on Terrorism, like the War on Poverty and the War on Drugs, is in so many ways just a tragic joke. But why Christians support any of these bogus "wars" is an even greater tragedy.

* * * * *

FALWELL'S FOLLY

Jerry Falwell has done it again. Just like Jacob's sons Simeon and Levi made him "stink among the inhabitants of the land" (Genesis 34:30), so Falwell has made Christians stink. Case in point—Falwell's recent *WorldNetDaily* article in which he made an attempt, and a very feeble one, to justify, with Scripture, President Bush's invasion of Iraq—an invasion which has resulted, and continues to result, in the senseless deaths of American servicemen. And if the article itself wasn't bad enough, he had the audacity to entitle it: "God is pro-war." As a Christian of the Independent Baptist persuasion (like Falwell), I am almost ashamed to identify myself as such. Although Falwell has been an embarrassment to Independent Baptists for years, his recent article is just too much to stomach.

Falwell is certainly correct when he says about war that "the Bible is not silent on the subject." Yes, it is true that "just as there are numerous references to peace in the Bible, there are frequent references to God-ordained war." And yes, it is true that Jesus is depicted in Revelation 19 as "bearing a 'sharp sword' and smiting nations, ruling them with 'a rod of iron.'" And yes again, it is true that "the Song of Victory in Exodus 15 hails God as a God of war." Furthermore, no one can deny that "God actually strengthened individuals for war, including Moses, Joshua, and many of the Old Testament judges who demonstrated great faith in battle." And finally, it is true that "the Bible tells us war will be a reality until Christ returns. And when the time is right, Jesus will indeed come again, ending all wars."

Falwell is also correct when he says about society that "we continue to live in violent times." And yes, "America continues to face the horrible realities of our fallen world. Suicide bombings and terrorist actions are beamed live into our homes daily."

The problem with Falwell's article is not with these observations that anyone who read the Bible and watched the nightly news already knew. The problem with the article is the numerous distortions of Scripture and the truth that occur in it.

Falwell's first distortion is the inappropriate use of that portion of Scripture that prefaces his article: "To every thing there is a season, and a time to every purpose under the heaven: A time to be born . . . , *a time of war.*" This implies that the present war in Iraq is just because, after all, there is "a time of war." If the United States was invaded then it would certainly be "a time of war." But it would be a morally justifiable defensive war against an aggressor. The war in Iraq is neither defensive nor against an aggressor.

Falwell's second distortion is the title of his article itself: "God is pro-war." To say that because God permitted wars to take place, and even commanded the nation of Israel in the Old Testament to conduct them, that he is "pro-war" is ludicrous. We know from the Bible that God is pro-holiness and pro-righteousness, but to say that God is "pro-war" doesn't sound like any description of God's attributes that I ever read in a systematic theology book. Was God pro-Crimean War? Was God pro-War of the Austrian Succession? Was God pro-War of the Roses? Whose side was he on in these conflicts? What Falwell really means is that God is pro-American wars. Falwell's shameless pseudo-patriotism is a violation of the third commandment in the Bible he professes to believe: "Thou shalt not take the name of the LORD thy God in vain" (Exodus 20:7).

Falwell's third distortion: "God even gives counsel to be wise in war. Proverbs 20:18: 'Every purpose is established by counsel: and with good advice make war.'" How this verse is supposed to mean that "God even gives counsel to be wise in war" is beyond me. Nothing in the verse or the context suggests that God is giving the counsel or the advice. Did God give Hitler and Stalin counsel to be wise in war? Did God give Pol Pot and Ho Chi Min advice to make war? Oh, I guess it just means that God only gives U.S. presidents counsel and advise to be wise in war? But could that even be the case? Did God give Lincoln counsel to invade the South after Lincoln said: "I have no purpose, directly or indirectly, to interfere with the institution of slavery in the States where it exists. I believe I have no lawful right to do so, and I have no inclination to do so."? Did God give advice to Wilson to make the world safe for democracy after Wilson sought reelection on the slogan "he kept us out of war"?

Falwell's fourth distortion: "It is apparent that our God-authored freedoms must be defended. Throughout the book of Judges, God calls the Israelites to go to war against the Midianites and Philistines. Why? Because these nations were trying to conquer Israel, and God's people were called to defend themselves." But what does invading Iraq have to do with defending our God-authored freedoms? For this analogy to be credible, several things must of necessity be true. First, Iraq would had to have been trying to conquer the United States—which it wasn't, and couldn't possibly have done so if it tried. Second, the citizens of the United States would have to be God's people—quite strange in view of the fact that God and his Bible are unwelcome in most of the country's schools. Christians can quote 2 Chronicles 7:14 all they want, but it still won't change the fact that America is not made up of God's people like Israel of the Old Testament. Third, invading another country would have to be a means of defending our God-authored freedoms. That is, we owe our freedoms to offensive wars by the United States military away from American soil in places that most

Americans couldn't locate on a map. And fourth, the state would have to be the defender of our God-given freedoms. But who has always been the greatest opponent of anyone's God-authored freedoms? Why, the state, of course.

Falwell's fifth distortion: "President Bush declared war in Iraq to defend innocent people. This is a worthy pursuit. In fact, Proverbs 21:15 tells us: 'It is joy to the just to do judgment: but destruction shall be to the workers of iniquity.'" Well, first of all, according to that archaic, neglected document in Washington known as the Constitution, the power to declare war belongs exclusively to Congress (Art. I, Sec. 8, Par. 11). The fact that Congress hasn't officially issued a declaration of war since World War II doesn't change anything. It only demonstrates that the Iraq fiasco is not any more constitutional than the Korea or Vietnam fiascos were. Secondly, I thought the war was all about finding weapons of mass destruction, destroying chemical weapons labs, or uncovering Iraq's nascent nuclear capability? If the United States is so interested in defending innocent people in Iraq then why was not Saddam Hussein removed during the First Gulf War? Why let them suffer all these years? And why stop at Iraq? Why not defend the innocent people in North Korea who have suffered under oppressive regimes for decades? And if it is such a worthy pursuit to defend innocent people in Iraq, then why not defend innocent people in America? How many millions of unborn children have been slaughtered in the United States since the 1973 *Roe v. Wade* decision? How many thousands of people are languishing in U.S. prisons for victimless crimes? There are also two problems with Falwell's equating the destruction of Iraq by the U.S. Military with the destruction of the workers of iniquity. First off, I don't recall reading in Proverbs that it is the job of the United States to destroy the workers of iniquity. And second, if "destruction shall be to the workers of iniquity," then the United States is in trouble, for we have worked iniquity all over the globe for the past fifty years.

Falwell's sixth distortion: "One of the primary purposes of the church is to stop the spread of evil, even at the cost of human lives. If we do not stop the spread of evil, many innocent lives will be lost and the kingdom of God suffers." I thought one of the primary purposes of the church was to preach the gospel? I thought one of the primary purposes of the church was to teach converts? There is no mention anywhere in the New Testament of the church being commanded to stop the spread of evil. Only God himself can stop the spread of evil. The Apostle Paul preached the gospel and taught converts (Acts 14:21), he didn't waste five minutes trying to stop the spread of something as nebulous as evil. And then there is the "cost of human lives." Should the church practice evil to stop evil? Does the end justify the means? Falwell apparently thinks it does, even though the Apostle Paul said it was slanderously reported that he was saying: "Let us do evil, that good may come?" (Romans 3:8). Falwell's attitude is like the then U.S. ambassador to the United Nations, Madeleine Albright, in 1996, saying that the deaths of 500,000 Iraqi children because of U.S. sanctions was "worth it" in order to punish Saddam Hussein.

Falwell's seventh distortion: "Some reading this column will surely ask, 'Doesn't the sixth commandment say, "Thou shalt not kill?"' Actually, no; it says: 'Thou shalt not commit murder.' There is a difference between killing and murdering. In fact, many times God commanded capital punishment for those who break the law." Falwell is exactly right, there is a difference between killing and murdering. The question then is this: Is dropping bombs on countries thousands of miles away for dubious reasons killing or murdering? I think the answer is quite obvious.

In addition to mentioning war, the writer of Ecclesiastes also says that there is "a time to keep silence" (Ecclesiastes 3:7). Mr. Falwell, are you listening?

* * * * *

SHOULD A CHRISTIAN JOIN THE MILITARY?

Christian enthusiasm for war is at an all-time high. Gullible Christians have not just tolerated the state's nebulous crusade against "evil," they have actively promoted both it and the overgrown U.S. Military establishment. Because the Republican Party is in control of the federal government instead of the "ungodly" Democrats, because President Bush is the commander in chief instead of the "immoral" Bill Clinton, and because the "enemy" is the easily-vilifiable Muslim infidel, many Christians, who certainly ought to know better given the history of state-sponsored persecution of Christians, "heretics," and other religious groups over the past two thousand years, have come to view the state, and in particular its coercive arm, the military, as sacrosanct.

For far too long Christians have turned a blind eye to the U.S. Global Empire of troops and bases that encircles the world. Many Christians have willingly served as cannon fodder for the state and its wars and military interventions. Christians who haven't died (wasted their life) for their country in some overseas desert or jungle increasingly perpetuate the myth that being a soldier in the U.S. Military is a noble occupation that one can wholeheartedly perform as a Christian.

The Question

The question of whether a Christian should join the military is a controversial one in some Christian circles. By a Christian I don't just mean someone who accepts the title by default because he was born in "Christian" America or "Christian" Europe. In this respect, everyone but Jews and atheists could be classified as Christians. The mention of a Christian in this article should be taken in the narrower sense of someone who professes to believe that Jesus Christ is the Saviour (Luke 2:11) and that the Bible is some kind of an authority (Acts 17:11). It is true that this may be too broad a definition for some Christians, and it is also true that many who profess to be Christians hold defective views on the person of Christ and the nature of the Atonement. But for the purposes of this article, the "broadness" of this definition and the permitting of these "defects" do not in any way affect the question: Should a

Christian join the military? In fact, the narrower one's definition of what constitutes a real Christian, the stronger the case can be made against a Christian joining the military.

The idea that there are certain things Christians should not do is not only scriptural (1 Corinthians 6:9-11; Galatians 5:19-21), it is readily acknowledged by Christians and non-Christians alike. Christians have historically applied this idea to occupations as well. But it is not just unlawful occupations like pimp, prostitute, drug dealer, and hit man that Christians have shied away from. Most Americans—whether they be atheist or theist—would have a problem with those occupations as well. Everyone knows that there are also certain lawful occupations that Christians frown upon: bartender, exotic dancer, casino card dealer, etc. This prohibition is also usually extended to benign occupations in not so benign environments. Therefore, a clerk in a drug store or grocery store is acceptable, but a clerk in liquor store or an x-rated video store is not. Likewise, most Christians would not work for an abortion clinic, for any amount of money, whether in the capacity of a doctor or a secretary. In other places of employment, however, a Christian might have no problem with being employed, only with working in a certain capacity. This explains why some Christians might not wait tables in restaurants that forced them to serve alcohol, but would feel perfectly comfortable working for the same restaurant in some other capacity, like a bookkeeper or janitor.

The larger question of whether a Christian (or anyone opposed to the federal leviathan) should work for the state is not at issue. Someone employed by the state as a teacher, a mailman, a security guard, or a park ranger is providing a lawful, moral, non-aggressive, non-intrusive service that is in the same manner also provided by the free market. Thus, it might be argued that working for the BATF, the CIA, the FBI, or as a regulation-enforcing federal bureaucrat is off limits, whereas these other occupations are not. The question then is which of these two groups the U.S. Military belongs in. Given the actions of the U.S. Military since Sherman's state-sponsored "total war" against Southerners and Indians, the host of twentieth-century interventions, subjugations, and "liberations," and the current debacle in Iraq, it should be obvious.

The question before us then is whether a Christian should join the military. Although my remarks are primarily directed at the idea of a Christian being a professional soldier (a hired assassin in some cases) for the state, they are also applicable to serving in the military in any capacity.

To save some people the trouble of e-mailing me to ask if I have ever been in the military, I will say now that, no, I have never been in the military. For some strange reason, many Americans think that if you have not "served" your country in the military then you have no right to criticize it. There are three problems with this attitude.

First of all, this is like saying that if you have not "served" in the Mafia then you have no right to criticize John Gotti. It reminds me of fellow travelers in the 1950s, 1960s, and 1970s saying that if you have not lived in the Soviet Union then you have no right to criticize it. So no, I am not a veteran, but I have family members who were in the military and have lived near military bases and been intimately associated with military personnel since I was ten years old. No, I am not a veteran, but I am a student of history ("Those who cannot learn from history are doomed to repeat it"—George Santayana), and was born with enough common sense to know government propaganda when I see it. I can also read above a tenth-grade level, which is about all it takes to compare the wisdom of the Founding Fathers with the drivel from Bush, Cheney, Wolfowitz, Powell, and Rumsfeld.

Secondly, some of the most vocal critics of the military have been in the military, like USMC Major General Smedley Butler. So it is not just non-veterans who are critics of the military.

The third problem with the knee-jerk reaction to this article and me because I have never been in the military is that it is misplaced indignation. I am only examining the question of whether a Christian should join the military. Criticism of the military is not my direct purpose.

Another objection to an article of this nature is that if it were not for the U.S. Military then no one would have the freedom right now to write anything. But if the military exists to defend our freedoms, and does not just function as the force behind an aggressive, interventionist U.S. foreign policy, then why are our troops scattered across 150 different regions of the world? Why doesn't the military control our borders? Why do we need a Department of Homeland Security if we already have a Department of Defense? Why, with the biggest military budget ever do we have less freedom in America now than at any time in history? The U.S. Military could not even defend the Pentagon. The case could even be argued that U.S. Military intervention is the cause for much of the anti-American sentiment in the world. So, like Brad Edmonds, I don't owe and still do not owe the military anything. I trust in God Almighty to keep me safe from a nuclear attack, not the U.S. Military.

The Commandments

Using the Ten Commandments (Exodus 20:3-17) as a guide, it is my contention that the military is no place for a Christian. As a Christian under the authority of the New Testament, I am perfectly aware that the Ten Commandments are in the Old Testament and were originally given to the nation of Israel. But I am also cognizant that the Apostle Paul said: "Whatsoever things were written aforetime were written for our learning" (Romans 15:4) after he had just recited many of the Ten Commandments (Romans 13:8–9).

1. Thou shalt have no other gods before me (Exodus 20:3).

The state has historically been the greatest enemy of Christianity. Yet, many Christians in the military have made the state their god. Members of the military are totally dependent on the state for their food, clothing, shelter, recreation, and medical care. They are conditioned to look to the state for their every need. But the state demands unconditional obedience. Shoot this person, bomb this city, blow up this building—don't ask why, just do it because the state tells you to. The soldier is conditioned to believe that whatever he does is right because it is done in the name of the state. The state's acts of aggression are regarded as acts of benevolence. Then, once the benevolent state is viewed as never doing anything wrong, it in essence becomes the all-seeing, all-knowing, omniscient state, since it would take absolute knowledge to know for certain that the person shot, the city bombed, or the building blown up "deserved" it.

2. Thou shalt not make unto thee any graven image (Exodus 20:4).

The state has an image that it expects its citizens to reverence and pledge allegiance to. This is especially true of people serving in the military. Perhaps the most famous picture of the flag is the raising of the flag by U.S. troops at Iwo Jima on February 23, 1945. But there is another picture of the flag that has occurred thousands of times that the state does its best to suppress: the picture of the flag-draped coffin of a life wasted in the service of one of the state's needless wars. Foreigners who object to our intervention in their country and our military presence across the globe burn American flags in protest. But they are not protesting because we are capitalists who believe in liberty, freedom, and democracy and they do not share our values. Christians in the military must reverence what has often justly come to be viewed by most of the world as a symbol of oppression. They must also pledge their allegiance to it. Christians blindly recite the Pledge of Allegiance without even bothering to find out where it came from, what its author intended, and how the state uses it to instill loyalty to the state in the minds of its youth. Never mind that the author was a socialist Baptist minister, Francis Bellamy (1855-1932), who was forced to resign from his church in Boston because of his socialist ideas (like preaching on "Jesus the Socialist"). Never mind that the idea for Bellamy's pledge of allegiance was taken from Lincoln's oath of allegiance imposed on Southerners after the successful Northern invasion of the Southern states. Never mind that "republic for which" the flag "stands" was, in Bellamy's eyes, "the One Nation which the Civil War was fought to prove." The Pledge is an allegiance oath to the omnipotent, omniscient state. There is nothing inherently wrong with the United States having a flag, but it has been made into a graven image that no Christian, in the military or otherwise, should bow down to.

3. Thou shalt not take the name of the LORD thy God in vain (Exodus 20:7).

The state will tolerate God and religion as long as He and it can be used to legitimize the state. God's name is taken in vain when it is used to justify the state's wars and military interventions. Some Christians in the military envision themselves as modern-day crusaders warring against the Muslim infidel. Indeed, the president even termed his war on terrorism "this crusade." Others, all the way up to the commander in chief, invoke the name of God or His words in Scripture to give authority to their unconstitutional, unscriptural, and immoral military adventures. When a young Christian man (or woman, unfortunately) leaves home and joins the military he often learns to take God's name in vain in ways that he never could have imagined. There is a reason the old expression is "cuss like a sailor," not cuss like a mechanic, an accountant, or a fireman. Singing "God Bless America" while cognizant of the abortions, promiscuity, and pornography that curse America is taking God's name in vain. Likewise, military chaplains asking God to bless troops on their missions of death and destruction are taking God's name in vain. Many Christians were upset a few years ago when the 9th U.S. Circuit Court of Appeals (which covers Alaska, Arizona, California, Hawaii, Idaho, Montana, Nevada, Oregon, and Washington) tried to strike out the phrase "under God" from the Pledge of Allegiance (which was only added in 1954). They should have cheered instead, for even though the two federal judges (the decision was 2-1) who made the ridiculous ruling that the inclusion of the phrase "under

God" was an unconstitutional "endorsement of religion" ought to have their head examined, America is not a nation "under God," and to say that it is (as when one recites the Pledge of Allegiance), is the epitome of using God's name in vain.

4. Remember the sabbath day, to keep it holy (Exodus 20:8).

Although the sabbath day is technically the Jewish seventh day (Saturday) and not the Christian first day (Sunday), the basic principle is still the same. Christians the world over set aside the first day of the week to attend church services. Christians in the military are often deployed to some strange city or remote country for months at a time and are therefore forced to violate the precept of "not forsaking the assembling of ourselves together" (Hebrews 10:25). Defense consultant Josh Pollack, in his "Saudi Arabia and the United States, 1931-2002," has documented that during the early decades of the American troop presence in Saudi Arabia, Air Force chaplains were forbidden to wear Christian insignia or hold formal services. During the First Gulf War of Bush the Elder, the importation of Bibles for Christian troops was discouraged, and no alcohol was permitted to U.S. troops in accordance with Islamic Law.

5. Honour thy father and thy mother (Exodus 20:12).

It used to be thought that following one's father into the military was a noble thing that honored him. Thankfully, this is not so much the case anymore. Is it honoring to one's father and mother for a Christian to accept the state's amoral values that are taught in the military and reject the values learned from a Christian upbringing? The temptations in the military for a Christian young person away from home for the first time are very great. Joining the military is one of the surest ways for a Christian to dishonor his parents by associating with bad company and picking up bad habits. This is not to deny that some Christians who are well grounded in the Scriptures live an exemplary life while in the military and are a positive force for good. But see the next point.

6. Thou shalt not kill (Exodus 20:13).

This is perhaps the greatest reason for a Christian not to join the military. But there is a difference between killing and murdering. Under certain conditions, a Christian would be entirely justified in taking up arms to defend himself, his family, and his property against an aggressor. If America was attacked, Christians could in good conscience kill and maim enemy invaders. However, when was the United States ever in danger from Guatemala, Vietnam, Indonesia, Grenada, Panama, Kosovo, Cuba, Haiti, Afghanistan, Iraq, North Korea, or any of the other places where the United States has intervened militarily? How then can a Christian justify killing any of them on their own soil? The old adage, "Join the army, meet interesting people, kill them," is now just "join the army and kill them" since you can't meet anyone at 10,000 feet before you release your load of bombs. The U.S. Military turns men into callous killers. The D.C. sniper, Lee Harvey Oswald, and Timothy McVey all learned how to kill in the military. When a Christian in the military is faced with an order to kill, bomb, or destroy someone or something halfway around the world that he has never met or seen, and is no real threat to him, his family, or his country, there is really only one option: "We ought to obey God rather than men" (Acts 5:29).

7. Thou shalt not commit adultery (Exodus 20:14).

Human nature being what it is, the forcing of men and women together, especially for extended periods on Navy ships, has been the source of many broken marriages and unwanted pregnancies. Christians in the military also face incredible temptations when they are deployed overseas. In his seminal work *Blowback: The Costs and Consequences of American Empire*, Chalmers Johnson has described the network of bars, strip clubs, whorehouses, and VD clinics that surround U.S.

bases overseas. The former U.S. naval base at Subic Bay in the Philippines "had no industry nearby except for the 'entertainment' business, which supported approximately 55,000 prostitutes and a total of 2,182 registered establishments offering 'rest and recreation' to American servicemen." At the annual Cobra Gold joint military exercise in Thailand: "Some three thousand prostitutes wait for sailors and marines at the South Pattaya waterfront, close to Utapao air base." The prohibition in this commandment applies equally as well to men who are not married, for "whosoever looketh on a woman to lust after her hath committed adultery with her already in his heart" (Matthew 5:28).

8. Thou shalt not steal (Exodus 20:15).

Through its system of forced revenue collection (the income tax), the state is guilty of stealing untold trillions of dollars from working Americans. Very little of that money is spent for constitutionally authorized purposes. One of the largest expenditures of the state is its bloated military budget. Training, feeding, housing, transporting, paying, and arming thousands of troops all over the planet is a very expensive undertaking. Robert Higgs has estimated the true military budget in fiscal year 2004 to be about $695 billion. Besides being the recipient of stolen money, a Christian in the military may have to steal the lives of the sons and daughters of parents he has never met. He may have to steal land in foreign countries to build bases on. He certainly steals the resources of the countries he bombs. Christians in the military should heed the words of the Apostle Paul: "Let him that stole steal no more: but rather let him labour, working with his hands the thing which is good, that he may have to give to him that needeth" (Ephesians 4:28).

9. Thou shalt not bear false witness against thy neighbour (Exodus 20:16).

The state is the greatest bearer of false witness that there has ever been. The latest round of lies concerns the war in Iraq. Continual government lies about Iraq's supposed weapons of mass destruction, aluminum tubes, chemical and biological weapons, threat to the United States, tie to al Qaeda, and link to the September 11th attacks are the rule rather than the exception. The Christian in the military is supporting a lie and living a lie when he devotes his time and energy to supporting a U.S. war machine based on deception, disinformation, falsehood, and lies.

10. Thou shalt not covet (Exodus 20:17).

Young people generally join the military for the wrong motive. Bored, indecisive, in trouble, unemployed, seeking to get away from home—these are some of the reasons why young men and women join the military. But perhaps the greatest reason young people join the military today is because of covetousness. Recruitment slogans all emphasize how much money an enlistee can earn towards his college education. Then there are enlistment bonuses, free medical care, commissary and exchange shopping privileges, the lucrative retirement program, and the future "veterans preference" to help get that government job after retirement. But aside from money, some people covet an increase in prestige ("The few, the proud, the Marines"). Others covet the power that powerful weapons bring. Some Christian young people join the military because they are patriotic, loyal Americans who have been conditioned to think that they owe the state something ("Ask not what your country can do for you, but what you can do for your country"). Their patriotism is noble, but misdirected.

The Conclusion

Should a Christian join the military? Should anyone join the military? The U.S. Military, although officially called the Department of Defense, is the state's arm of aggression. If it limited itself to controlling our borders, patrolling our coasts, and protecting our citizens instead of intervening around the globe and leaving death and destruction in its wake then perhaps it might be a noble occupation for a Christian. But as it is now, the military is no place for a Christian.

The argument that you have to become one of them to win them is fallacious. No one would think of becoming a pimp or a prostitute in order to convert them to Christianity. The fact that a Christian is compared to a soldier (2 Timothy 2:3) is no more a scriptural endorsement of Christians in the military than God being compared to "a mighty man that shouteth by reason of wine" (Psalm 78:65) is an endorsement of drunkenness.

When the nation of Israel rejected the LORD and desired a king "like all the nations" (1 Samuel 8:5), God described "the manner of the king that shall reign over them" (1 Samuel 8:9):

> And he said, This will be the manner of the king that shall reign over you: He will take your sons, and appoint them for himself, for his chariots, and to be his horsemen; and some shall run before his chariots.
>
> And he will appoint him captains over thousands, and captains over fifties; and will set them to ear his ground, and to reap his harvest, and to make his instruments of war, and instruments of his chariots.
>
> And he will take your daughters to be confectionaries, and to be cooks, and to be bakers.
>
> And he will take your fields, and your vineyards, and your oliveyards, even the best of them, and give them to his servants.
>
> And he will take the tenth of your seed, and of your vineyards, and give to his officers, and to his servants.
>
> And he will take your menservants, and your maidservants, and your goodliest young men, and your asses, and put them to his work.
>
> He will take the tenth of your sheep: and ye shall be his servants.
>
> And ye shall cry out in that day because of your king which ye shall have chosen you; and the LORD will not hear you in that day.
>
> Nevertheless the people refused to obey the voice of

Samuel; and they said, Nay; but we will have a king over us;
That we also may be like all the nations; and that our king may judge us, and go out before us, and fight our battles (1 Samuel 8:11–20).

Christians should remember that "the weapons of our warfare are not carnal" (2 Corinthians 10:4), and that we wield "the sword of the spirit, which is the word of God" (Ephesians 6:17).

That criticizing the military or recommending that Christians don't join it is seen as being un-American or traitorous shows just how effective the state has been with its propaganda. The United States is the greatest country on earth for a Christian to live in, but in spite of its military, not because of it.

* * * * *

CHRISTIAN KILLERS?

There is no doubt that many of the soldiers responsible for the recent death and destruction in Fallujah are Christians. And there is no doubt that many Americans who call for more death and destruction in Iraq and elsewhere are Christians as well.

Christian Killers.

The phrase should be a contradiction in terms. If someone referred to Christian adulterers, Christian drug addicts, Christian prostitutes, Christian pimps, Christian gangsta rappers, or Christian acid rockers, most Christians would get an extremely perplexed look on their face. But when Christians in the military continue killing for the state, and Christians not in the military call for more killing in the name of the state, many Christians don't even raise an eyebrow.

In some respects, this is the fault of religious "leaders." Christians in the pew are in many cases just blindly following their pastors, priests, elders, and ministers who, instead of preaching the gospel, are preaching the same pro-war politics their congregation hears on the Sean Hannity radio show or else they are not denouncing the debacle in Iraq for what it is: unscriptural, immoral, and unconstitutional. Conservative religious leaders are in some cases nothing more than cheerleaders for George Bush and the Republican Party.

But even if a Christian hears nothing but pro-war propaganda from the pulpit, it is still no excuse, for Christians have access to the truth if they will just put forth the effort to look for it. They have a Bible they can read for themselves. They have the example of some principled Christian leaders who have opposed the debacle in Iraq from the beginning. They have an abundance of alternative news sources to receive information from besides the pro-war propaganda they get from the Fox War Channel and the *War Street Journal*. It is unfortunate that some Christians won't read anything unless it was written by some other Christian they know and usually agree with. God forbid that they should read something by someone outside of their denomination, circle, or "camp"—or even worse, someone they consider to be a nominal Christian or not a Christian at all.

To justify their consent or silence, and to keep their congregations in line, Christian leaders repeat to their parishioners the mantra of "obey the powers that be," a loose paraphrase of Romans 13:1, as if that somehow means that they should blindly follow whatever the president or the government says, and even worse, that it overturns the commandment "Thou shalt not kill" (Exodus 20:13; Deuteronomy 5:17), which is repeated in the New Testament (Matthew 19:18; Romans 13:9). The way some Christians repeat the "obey the powers that be" mantra, one would think that they would slit their own mothers' throats if the state told them to do so.

Under what circumstances, then, is a Christian justified in or excused from killing another human being? Is it ever all right for a Christian to be a "killer"? As I see it, there are four circumstances under which a Christian could justifiably kill or be excused from killing: capital punishment, self-defense, accidents, and "just" wars.

A Christian who *lawfully* carried out capital punishment would not be committing murder. Although the subject of capital punishment is sometimes hotly debated, the Bible sanctions it before the law (Genesis 9:6), under the law (Numbers 35:16-21, 30-31), and under the New Testament (Acts 25:11; Romans 13:4). For more on the death penalty see Walter Block.

No one, Christian or otherwise, would fault a man for killing another man in self-defense. Only the most diehard pacifist would refuse to act in self-defense if he was attacked. This would have to include the protection of one's family as well, for if the Bible condemns a Christian for not providing for his own house (1 Timothy 5:8), how could a Christian not ensure by whatever means necessary the protection of his family's life?

Accidents happen. And sometimes someone is tragically killed. This does not make the perpetrator a murderer. The Jews were commanded in the Old Testament to establish cities of refuge (Numbers 35:6, 11-15) to which someone might flee that killed his neighbor unawares or ignorantly (Numbers 35:11; Deuteronomy 19:4-5).

Most Christians would wholeheartedly agree with these first three propositions. The problem is with war; specifically, the fact that all wars are not created equal. The vast majority of wars in the world's history have been destructive, unjust, and immoral. What constitutes a just war is a question I have answered in the essay "Christianity and War." Obviously, an aggressive, preemptive war against a country with no navy or air force, an economy in ruins after a decade of sanctions, and that was no threat to the United States is not a just war.

A Christian fighting for the U.S. Government in Iraq doesn't fall under any of these circumstances.

After Bush launched his nebulous "war on terrorism" by having Afghanistan bombed back to the Stone Age to supposedly rid the world of Osama bin Laden, al-Qaeda, and the Taliban, he announced to the world his "axis of evil" and went to war against Iraq to, depending on what day it was, rid the world of the evil Saddam Hussein or because Iraq violated U.N. resolutions or to destroy Iraq's supposed stockpiles of weapons of mass destruction or because of the perceived connection between al-Qaeda and Iraq or to liberate the Iraqi people or to bring democracy to Iraq.

Christians who support or remain silent about Bush's "war against terrorism" are terribly inconsistent. If the state were to say: "Here Christian, put on this uniform, take this gun, go to your hometown, and kill your father," Christians would recoil in horror and refuse to obey the state. But if the state were to say: "Here Christian, put on this uniform, take this gun, go to Iraq, and kill someone else's father," I am afraid that many Christians would reply, "When does my plane leave?"

Why is it that the same Christian who would not do the former has no qualms about doing the latter?

Christians who voted for George W. Bush (even if it is true that he was in fact the lesser of two evils—a dubious proposition), or make excuses for his invasion of Iraq, are supporting a man with blood on his hands (Iraqi blood and American blood). The fact that the president himself never killed anyone is irrelevant—Adolf Hitler never gassed a single Jew.

What, then, is a Christian to do? What should any citizen do? Even though it is no longer posted in the public schools, most people know the answer: "Thou shalt not kill" (Exodus 20:13). Stop killing or supporting or making excuses for those who do. Quit ignoring the fact that the United States has a global empire of troops and bases that inevitably leads to more killing. Realize that it is the interventionist foreign policy of the United States that is the main reason why the world hates us. Acknowledge that the reason more countries don't hate us is because we bribe them with foreign aid (after the money is first confiscated from U.S. taxpayers).

It is true that the Bible commands the Christian: "Submit yourselves to every ordinance of man for the Lord's sake" (1 Peter 2:13). And it is true that it also says: "Let every soul be subject unto the higher powers" (Romans 13:1). But it doesn't take a seminary education to see that this doesn't trump the commandment: "Thou shalt not kill." To know when to submit and when to be in subjection, we have some relevant biblical examples to go by—two in the Old Testament book of Daniel and two in the New Testament book of Acts.

In Daniel chapter 3, we read that King Nebuchadnezzar "made an image of gold, whose height was threescore cubits, and the breadth thereof six cubits: he set it up in the plain of Dura, in the province of Babylon" (Daniel 3:1). It was then decreed that when the music started, everyone was to "fall down and worship the golden image that Nebuchadnezzar the king hath set up" (Daniel 3:5). The penalty for noncompliance was to be "cast into the midst of a burning fiery furnace" (Daniel 3:6). It was then charged that Shadrach, Meshach, and Abednego would not worship the golden image (Daniel 3:12). When brought before the king and threatened with being cast into the furnace, Shadrach, Meshach, and Abednego answered the king: "If it be so, our God whom we serve is able to deliver us from the burning fiery furnace, and he will deliver us out of thine hand, O king. But if not, be it known unto thee, O king, that we will not serve thy gods, nor worship the golden image which thou hast set up" (Daniel 3:17-18). Although Nebuchadnezzar did cast them into the furnace, and God did deliver them, the point is that these three Hebrews did not submit and were not subject to King Nebuchadnezzar.

In Daniel chapter 6, we read that King Darius made a decree that "whosoever shall ask a petition of any God or man for thirty days," except from the king, "shall be cast into the den of lions" (Daniel 6:7). But "when Daniel knew that the writing was signed, he went into his house; and his windows being open in his chamber toward Jerusalem, he kneeled upon his knees three times a day, and prayed, and gave thanks before his God, as he did aforetime" (Daniel 6:10). For his disobedience, Daniel was cast into the den of lions, but God delivered him. The point, however, is that Daniel did not submit and was not subject to King Darius.

In Acts chapter 4, the Apostles Peter and John were imprisoned by the leaders of the Jews and then brought before them and commanded "not to speak at all nor teach in the name of Jesus" (Acts 4:18). But instead of submitting and being in subjection, they replied: "Whether it be right in the sight of God to hearken unto you more than unto God, judge ye. For we cannot but speak the things which we have seen and heard" (Acts 4:19-20). They even prayed for boldness to continue speaking (Acts 4:29).

In Acts chapter 5, some apostles were put in prison by order of the high priest (Acts 5:17-18). They were freed by an angel and ordered to "stand and speak in the temple to the people all the words of this life" (Acts 5:20). These apostles were then brought before the leaders of the Jews and asked: "Did not we straitly command you that ye should not teach in this name? And, behold, ye have filled Jerusalem with your doctrine, and intend to bring this man's blood upon us" (Acts 5:28). But rather than apologizing and submitting and being subject to them, the apostles replied: "We ought to obey God rather than men" (Acts 5:29).

To say, as some Christians do, that because "The LORD is a man of war" (Exodus 15:3), and God allows wars between nations, that it is honorable for Christians to enthusiastically participate in U.S. wars of aggression is about the most profound demonstration of biblical ignorance that one could manifest.

Perhaps I should close by saying that I have never advocated, nor am I now advocating, nor do I intend to advocate in the future, any armed resistance to the government or any aggression against the government in any way. The pen is mightier than the sword. "The weapons of our warfare are not carnal" (2 Corinthians 10:4). However, as Thomas Jefferson said in the Declaration of Independence:

> We hold these truths to be self-evident, that all men are created equal, that they are endowed by their Creator with certain unalienable rights, that among these are life, liberty and the pursuit of happiness. That to secure these rights, governments are instituted among men, deriving their just powers from the consent of the governed. That whenever any form of government becomes destructive to these ends, it is the right of the people to alter or to abolish it, and to institute new government, laying its foundation on such

principles and organizing its powers in such form, as to them shall seem most likely to effect their safety and happiness. Prudence, indeed, will dictate that governments long established should not be changed for light and transient causes; and accordingly all experience hath shown that mankind are more disposed to suffer, while evils are sufferable, than to right themselves by abolishing the forms to which they are accustomed. But when a long train of abuses and usurpations, pursuing invariably the same object evinces a design to reduce them under absolute despotism, it is their right, it is their duty, to throw off such government, and to provide new guards for their future security.

And, as even Abraham Lincoln said (long before his invasion of the Southern states):

Any people anywhere, being inclined and having the power, have the right to rise up and shake off the existing government, and form a new one that suits them better. This is a most valuable, a most sacred right—a right which we hope and believe is to liberate the world.

What is a Christian (or anyone) going to do when he faces God at the Judgment and has to give an account of his actions? Suppose he is asked a simple question: "Why did you kill those people defending their homes in Iraq?" And suppose he replied: "Because the U.S. government told me to." What do you suppose would be the Lord's reaction to such a reply? But what else could a man say? He could not say that the United States was under attack. He could not say that Iraq was a threat to the United States. He could not say that he was protecting his family. He could not say that he was protecting his property. He could not even legitimately say that he was protecting himself, since he was in fact a trespasser on someone else's property intending to do the owner great bodily harm.

"Cursed be he that taketh reward to slay an innocent person. And all the people shall say, Amen" (Deuteronomy 27:25).

* * * * *

BRUTUS ON THE EVILS OF STANDING ARMIES

Recognizing his friend Brutus among his assassins, Julius Caesar (in the words of William Shakespeare) uttered the immortal phrase "Et tu, Brute? "This Latin sentence meaning "Even you, Brutus?" is the only Brutus that most Americans have ever heard of.

But whether one has heard of Brutus from the study of Shakespeare's play Julius Caesar or from a World history course, there is a Brutus in American history that most Americans have never heard of.

The Brutus of American history is one of the forgotten Anti-Federalists. It was their principled opposition to the Constitution that led to the adoption of the Bill of Rights. But because the Federalists prevailed, the writings of the Anti-Federalists have largely been forgotten.

Every student of American government has studied the eighty-five essays written between October 1787 and August 1788 in favor of the adoption of the new Constitution. Known collectively as *The Federalist*, they were all signed Publius (after the ancient Roman statesman), but authored by Alexander Hamilton, James Madison, and John Jay.

Brutus was the name signed to sixteen essays written in opposition to the new Constitution replacing the Articles of Confederation. They were all published in the *New York Journal* from October 1787 to April 1788. None of the essays have titles, and most were addressed to the people or the citizens of the State of New York. The first essay of Brutus actually appeared nine days before the first essay of *The Federalist*. The essays signed Brutus are generally ascribed to Robert Yates (1738–1801), a New York judge who served on the committee that drafted the first constitution for New York State. Yates, along with John Lansing (1754–1829) and Alexander Hamilton, was a delegate to the Constitutional Convention in Philadelphia. Yates and Lansing withdrew from the Convention early and opposed the adoption of the Constitution by the state of New

York.

One subject that Brutus speaks on at length is the evils of standing armies. In four of his sixteen essays (numbers 1, 8, 9, 10), he explains how the establishment and maintenance of standing armies breeds fear, is destructive to liberty, and should be viewed as a scourge to a country instead of a benefit.

On the subject of war itself, Brutus believed that only a defensive war was justifiable. He recognized that the countries of Europe were plagued by destructive wars:

> The European governments are almost all of them framed, and administered with a view to arms, and war, as that in which their chief glory consists; they mistake the end of government—it was designed to save mens lives, not to destroy them. We ought to furnish the world with an example of a great people, who in their civil institutions hold chiefly in view, the attainment of virtue, and happiness among ourselves. Let the monarchs, in Europe, share among them the glory of depopulating countries, and butchering thousands of their innocent citizens, to revenge private quarrels, or to punish an insult offered to a wife, a mistress, or a favorite: I envy them not the honor, and I pray heaven this country may never be ambitious of it. The czar Peter the great, acquired great glory by his arms; but all this was nothing, compared with the true glory which he obtained, by civilizing his rude and barbarous subjects, diffusing among them knowledge, and establishing, and cultivating the arts of life: by the former he desolated countries, and drenched the earth with human blood: by the latter he softened the ferocious nature of his people, and pointed them to the means of human happiness.

In his first essay, Brutus brings up the subject of standing armies in his discussion of the dangers of a consolidated central government over a large territorial republic:

> It might be here shown, that the power of the federal legislative, to raise and support armies at pleasure, as well in peace as in war, and their controul over the militia, tend,

not only to a consolidation of the government, but the destruction of liberty.

In despotic governments, as well as in all the monarchies of Europe, standing armies are kept up to execute the commands of the prince or the magistrate, and are employed for this purpose when occasion requires: But they have always proved the destruction of liberty, and [as] abhorrent to the spirit of a free republic. In England, where they depend upon the parliament for their annual support, they have always been complained of as oppressive and unconstitutional, and are seldom employed in executing of the laws; never except on extraordinary occasions, and then under the direction of a civil magistrate.

A free republic will never keep a standing army to execute its laws. It must depend upon the support of its citizens. But when a government is to receive its support from the aid of the citizens, it must be so constructed as to have the confidence, respect, and affection of the people. Men who, upon the call of the magistrate, offer themselves to execute the laws, are influenced to do it either by affection to the government, or from fear; where a standing army is at hand to punish offenders, every man is actuated by the latter principle, and therefore, when the magistrate casts, will obey: but, where this is not the case, the government must rest for its support upon the confidence and respect which the people have for their government and laws.

He concludes that if the people have "no confidence in their legislature, suspect them of ambitious views, be jealous of every measure they adopt, and will not support the laws they pass," then the government will be "nerveless and inefficient, and no way will be left to render it otherwise, but by establishing an armed force to execute the laws at the point of the bayonet—a government of all others the most to be dreaded."

In his eighth essay, Brutus raises the subject of standing armies in his discussion of the new federal government being authorized to raise and support armies:

Let us then enquire, whether standing armies in time of peace, would be ever beneficial to our country—or if in some extraordinary cases, they might be necessary; whether it is not true, that they have generally proved a scourge to a country, and destructive of their liberty.

He then reprints the text of a speech against standing armies recently delivered in the British Parliament, because, as he says, it "is so full to the point, and so much better than any thing I can say":

"I have always been, and always shall be against a standing army of any kind; to me it is a terrible thing, whether under that of a parliamentary, or any other designation; a standing army is still a standing army by whatever name it is called; they are a body of men distinct from the body of the people; they are governed by different laws, and blind obedience, and an entire submission to the orders of their commanding officer, is their only principle; the nations around us, sir, are already enslaved, and have been enslaved by those very means; by means of their standing armies they have every one lost their liberties; it is indeed impossible that the liberties of the people in any country can be preserved where a numerous standing army is kept up. Shall we then take our measures from the example of our neighbours? No, sir, on the contrary, from their misfortunes we ought to learn to avoid those rocks upon which they have split."

"It signifies nothing to tell me that our army is commanded by such gentlemen as cannot be supposed to join in any measures for enslaving their country; it may be so; I have a very good opinion of many gentlemen now in the army; I believe they would not join in any such measures; but their lives are uncertain, nor can we be sure how long they will be kept in command, they may all be dismissed in a moment, and proper tools of power put in their room. Besides, sir, we know the passions of men, we know how dangerous it is to trust the best of men with too much power. Where was a braver army than that under Jul. Caesar? Where was there ever an army that had served their country more faithfully? That army was commanded generally by the best citizens of Rome, by men of great fortune and figure in their country, yet that army enslaved their country. The affections of the soldiers towards their country, the honor and integrity of the under officers, are not to be depended on. By the military law the administration of justice is so quick, and the punishment so severe, that neither the officer nor soldier dare dispute the orders of his supreme commander; he must not consult his own inclination. If an officer were commanded to pull his own father out of this house, he must do it; he dares not disobey; immediate death would be the sure consequence of the least grumbling: and if an officer were sent into the court of request, accompanied by a body of musketeers with screwed bayonets, and with orders to tell us what we ought to do, and how we were to vote: I know what would be the duty of this house; I know it would be our duty to order the officer to be hanged at the door of the lobby; but I doubt, sir, I doubt much, if such a spirit could be found in the house, or in any house of commons that will ever be in England."

"Sir, I talk not of imaginary things? I talk of what has happened to an English house of commons, from an English army; not only from an English army, but an army that was raised by that very house of commons, an army that was paid by them, and an army that was commanded by generals appointed by them; therefore do not let us vainly imagine, that an army, raised and maintained by authority of parliament, will always be so submissive to them. If an army be so numerous as to have it in their power to overawe the parliament, they will be submissive as long as the parliament does nothing to disoblige their favourite general; but when that case happens, I am afraid, that in place of the parliament's dismissing the army, the army will dismiss the parliament."

Brutus concludes from this speech that "if this great man's reasoning be just, it follows, that keeping up a standing army, would be in the highest degree dangerous to the liberty and happiness of the community—and if so, the general government ought not to have authority to do it; for no government should be empowered to do that which if done, would tend to destroy public liberty."

In his ninth essay, Brutus faults the proposed constitution for its lack of a bill of rights. He acknowledges that the framers of the new constitution believed in prohibiting or restricting the general government from exercising certain powers. Nevertheless, he wonders why, if there are sections in the proposed constitution that prohibit bills of attainder and restrict the suspension of the writ of habeas corpus, that there is no prohibition or restriction against standing armies since they are likewise just as harmful:

> Let us apply these remarks to the case of standing armies in times of peace. If they generally prove the destruction of the happiness and libertys of the people, the legislature ought not to have power to keep them up, or if they had, this power should be so restricted, as to secure the people against the danger arising from the exercise of it.

> That standing armies are dangerous to the liberties of a people was proved in my last number—If it was necessary, the truth of the position might be confirmed by the history of almost every nation in the world. A cloud of the most illustrious patriots of every age and country, where freedom has been enjoyed, might be adduced as witnesses in support of the sentiment. But I presume it would be useless, to enter into a laboured argument, to prove to the people of America, a position, which has so long and so generally been received by them as a kind of axiom.

> Some of the advocates for this new system controvert this sentiment, as they do almost every other that has been maintained by the best writers on free government.— Others, though they will not expressly deny, that standing armies in times of peace are dangerous, yet join with these in maintaining, that it is proper the general government

should be vested with the power to do it. I shall now proceed to examine the arguments they adduce in support of their opinions.

A writer, in favor of this system, treats this objection as a ridiculous one. He supposes it would be as proper to provide against the introduction of Turkish janizaries, or against making the Alcoran a rule of faith.

But, why is this provision so ridiculous? because, says this author, it is unnecessary. But, why is it unnecessary? ["]because, the principles and habits, as well as the power of the Americans are directly opposed to standing armies; and there is as little necessity to guard against them by positive constitutions, as to prohibit the establishment of the Mahometan religion." It is admitted then, that a standing army in time of peace, is an evil. I ask then, why should this government be authorised to do evil? If the principles and habits of the people of this country are opposed to standing armies in time of peace, if they do not contribute to the public good, but would endanger the public liber[ty] and happiness, why should the government be [vested] with the power? No reason can be given, why [rulers] should be authorised to do, what, if done, would oppose the principles and habits of the people, and endanger the public safety, but there is every reason in the world, that they should be prohibited from the exercise of such a power. But this author supposes, that no danger is to be apprehended from the exercise of this power, because, if armies are kept up, it will be by the people themselves, and therefore, to provide against it, would be as absurd as for a man to "pass a law in his family, that no troops should be quartered in his family by his consent." This reasoning supposes, that the general government is to be exercised by the people of America themselves—But such an idea is groundless and absurd. There is surely a distinction between the people and their rulers, even when the latter are representatives of the former.—They certainly are not identically the same, and it cannot be disputed, but it may and often does happen, that they do not possess the same sentiments or pursue the same interests. I think I have shewn, that as this government is constituted, there is little reason to expect, that the interest of the people and their rulers will be the same.

The idea that there is no danger of the establishment of a standing army, under the new constitution, is without foundation.

It is a well known fact, that a number of those who had an agency in producing this system, and many of those who it is probable will have a principal share in the administration of the government under it, if it is adopted, are avowedly in favour of standing armies. It is a language common among them, "That no people can be kept in order, unless the government have an army to awe them into obedience; it is necessary to support the dignity of government, to have a military establishment." And there will not be wanting a variety of plausible reason to justify the raising one, drawn from the danger we are in from the Indians on our frontiers, or from the European provinces in our neighbourhood. If to this we add, that an army will afford a decent support, and agreeable employment to the young men of many families, who are too indolent to follow occupations that will require care and industry, and too poor to live without doing any business we can have little reason to doubt, but that we shall have a large standing army, as soon as this government can find money to pay them, and perhaps sooner.

Brutus then directly engages Hamilton, who had written several essays in *The Federalist* trying to answer objections to standing armies:

A writer, who is the boast of the advocates of this new constitution, has taken great pains to shew, that this power was proper and necessary to be vested in the general government.

He first attempts to shew, that this objection is futile and disingenuous, because the power to keep up standing armies, in time of peace, is vested, under the present government, in the legislature of every state in the union, except two. Now this is so far from being true, that it is expressly declared, by the present articles of confederation, that no body of forces "shall be kept up by any state, in time of peace, except such number only, as in the judgment of the United States in Congress assembled, shall be deemed requisite to garrison the forts necessary for the defence of such state." Now, was it candid and ingenuous to endeavour to persuade the public, that the general government had no other power than your own legislature have on this head; when the truth is, your legislature have no authority to raise and keep up any forces?

He next tells us, that the power given by this constitution, on this head, is similar to that which Congress possess under the present confederation. As little ingenuity is manifested in this representation as in that of the former.

I shall not undertake to enquire whether or not Congress are vested with a power to keep up a standing army in time of peace; it has been a subject warmly debated in Congress, more than once, since the peace; and one of the most respectable states in the union, were so fully convinced that they had no such power, that they expressly instructed their delegates to enter a solemn protest against it on the journals of Congress, should they attempt to exercise it.

But should it be admitted that they have the power, there is such a striking dissimilarity between the restrictions under which the present Congress can exercise it, and that of the proposed government, that the comparison will serve rather to shew the impropriety of vesting the proposed government with the power, than of justifying it.

It is acknowledged by this writer, that the powers of Congress, under the present confederation, amount to little more than that of recommending. If they determine to raise troops, they are obliged to effect it through the authority of the state legislatures. This will, in the first instance, be a most powerful restraint upon them, against ordering troops to be raised. But if they should vote an army, contrary to the opinion and wishes of the people, the legislatures of the respective states would not raise them. Besides, the present Congress hold their places at the will and pleasure of the legislatures of the states who send them, and no troops can be raised, but by the assent of nine states out of the thirteen. Compare the power proposed to be lodged in the legislature on this head, under this constitution, with that vested in the present Congress, and every person of the least discernment, whose understanding is not totally blinded by prejudice, will perceive, that they bear no analogy to each other. Under the present confederation, the representatives of nine states, out of thirteen, must assent to the raising of troops, or they cannot be levied: under the proposed constitution, a less number than the representatives of two states, in the house of representatives, and the representatives of three states and an half in the senate, with the assent of the president, may raise any number of troops they please. The present Congress are restrained from an undue exercise of this power, from this consideration, they know the state legislatures, through whose authority it must be carried into effect, would not comply with the requisition for the purpose, if it was evidently opposed to the public good: the proposed constitution authorizes the legislature to carry their determinations into execution, without the intervention of any other body between them and the people.

In his tenth essay, which is devoted exclusively to the evils of standing armies, Brutus begins with a discussion of how a standing army can subvert the very government whose authority it is supposed to be under:

The liberties of a people are in danger from a large standing army, not only because the rulers may employ them for the purposes of supporting themselves in any usurpations of power, which they may see proper to exercise, but there is great hazard, that an army will subvert the forms of the government, under whose authority, they are raised, and establish one, according to the pleasure of their leader.

To prove his point, he then adduces the historical examples of Rome and Britain:

> We are informed, in the faithful pages of history, of such events frequently happening.—Two instances have been mentioned in a former paper. They are so remarkable, that they are worthy of the most careful attention of every lover of freedom.—They are taken from the history of the two most powerful nations that have ever existed in the world; and who are the most renowned, for the freedom they enjoyed, and the excellency of their constitutions:—I mean Rome and Britain.
>
> In the first, the liberties of the commonwealth was destroyed, and the constitution overturned, by an army, lead by Julius Cesar, who was appointed to the command, by the constitutional authority of that commonwealth. He changed it from a free republic, whose fame had sounded, and is still celebrated by all the world, into that of the most absolute despotism. A standing army effected this change, and a standing army supported it through a succession of ages, which are marked in the annals of history, with the most horrid cruelties, bloodshed, and carnage;—The most devilish, beastly, and unnatural vices, that ever punished or disgraced human nature.
>
> The same army, that in Britain, vindicated the liberties of that people from the encroachments and despotism of a tyrant king, assisted Cromwell, their General, in wresting from the people, that liberty they had so dearly earned.
>
> You may be told, these instances will not apply to our case.—But those who would persuade you to believe this, either mean to deceive you, or have not themselves considered the subject.

Continuing his argument, Brutus contrasts Caesar and Cromwell with George Washington:

> I firmly believe, no country in the world had ever a more

patriotic army, than the one which so ably served this country, in the late war.

But had the General who commanded them, been possessed of the spirit of a Julius Cesar or a Cromwell, the liberties of this country, had in all probability, terminated with the war; or had they been maintained, might have cost more blood and treasure, than was expended in the conflict with Great-Britain. When an anonimous writer addressed the officers of the army at the close of the war, advising them not to part with their arms, until justice was done them— the effect it had is well known. It affected them like an electric shock. He wrote like Cesar; and had the commander in chief, and a few more officers of rank, countenanced the measure, the desperate resolution had been taken, to refuse to disband. What the consequences of such a determination would have been, heaven only knows.— The army were in the full vigor of health and spirits, in the habit of discipline, and possessed of all our military stores and apparatus. They would have acquired great accessions of strength from the country.—Those who were disgusted at our republican forms of government (for such there then were, of high rank among us) would have lent them all their aid.—We should in all probability have seen a constitution and laws, dictated to us, at the head of an army, and at the point of a bayonet, and the liberties for which we had so severely struggled, snatched from us in a moment. It remains a secret, yet to be revealed, whether this measure was not suggested, or at least countenanced, by some, who have had great influence in producing the present system. —Fortunately indeed for this country, it had at the head of the army, a patriot as well as a general; and many of our principal officers, had not abandoned the characters of citizens, by assuming that of soldiers, and therefore, the scheme proved abortive. But are we to expect, that this will always be the case? Are we so much better than the people of other ages and of other countries, that the same allurements of power and greatness, which led them aside from their duty, will have no influence upon men in our country? Such an idea, is wild and extravagant.—Had we indulged such a delusion, enough has appeared in a little time past, to convince the most credulous, that the passion for pomp, power and greatness, works as powerfully in the hearts of many of our better sort, as it ever did in any country under heaven.—Were the same opportunity again to offer, we should very probably be grossly disappointed, if we made dependence, that all who then rejected the overture, would do it again.

Brutus concludes:

From these remarks, it appears, that the evil to be feared from a large standing army in time of peace, does not arise solely from the apprehension, that the rulers may employ them for the purpose of promoting their own ambitious views, but that equal, and perhaps greater danger, is to be apprehended from their overturning the constitutional powers of the government, and assuming the power to dictate any form they please.

Brutus again directly engages Hamilton, who had argued in *The Federalist* that we needed a standing army in peacetime to guard against Indians and to repel an invasion from abroad:

The advocates for power, in support of this right in the proposed government, urge that a restraint upon the discretion of the legislatures, in respect to military establish-ments in time of peace, would be improper to be imposed, because they say, it will be necessary to maintain small garrisons on the frontiers, to guard against the depredations of the Indians, and to be prepared to repel any encroach-ments or invasions that may be made by Spain or Britain.

The amount of this argument striped of the abundant verbages with which the author has dressed it, is this:

It will probably be necessary to keep up a small body of troops to garrison a few posts, which it will be necessary to maintain, in order to guard against the sudden encroach-ments of the Indians, or of the Spaniards and British; and therefore, the general government ought to be invested with power to raise and keep up a standing army in time of peace, without restraint; at their discretion.

I confess, I cannot perceive that the conclusion follows from the premises. Logicians say, it is not good reasoning to infer a general conclusion from particular premises: though I am not much of a Logician, it seems to me, this argument is very like that species of reasoning.

When the patriots in the parliament in Great-Britain, contended with such force of argument, and all the powers of eloquence, against keeping up standing armies in time of peace, it is obvious, they never entertained an idea, that small garrisons on their frontiers, or in the neighbourhood of powers, from whom they were in danger of encroachments, or guards, to take care of public arsenals would thereby be prohibited.

The advocates for this power farther urge that it is necessary, because it may, and probably will happen, that circumstances will render it requisite to raise an army to be prepared to repel attacks of an enemy, before a formal declaration of war, which in modern times has fallen into disuse. If the constitution prohibited the raising an army, until a war actually commenced, it would deprive the government of the power of providing for the defence of the country, until the enemy were within our territory. If the restriction is not to extend to the raising armies in cases of emergency, but only to the keeping them up, this would leave the matter to the discretion of the legislature; and they might, under the pretence that there was danger of an invasion, keep up the army as long as they judged proper— and hence it is inferred, that the legislature should have authority to raise and keep up an army without any restriction. But from these premises nothing more will follow than this, that the legislature should not be so restrained, as to put it out of their power to raise an army, when such exigencies as are instanced shall arise. But it does not thence follow, that the government should be empowered to raise and maintain standing armies at their discretion as well in peace as in war. If indeed, it is impossible to vest the general government with the power of raising troops to garrison the frontier posts, to guard arsenals, or to be prepared to repel an attack, when we saw a power preparing to make one, without giving them a general and indefinite authority, to raise and keep up armies, without any restriction or qualification, then this reasoning might have weight; but this has not been proved nor can it be.

It is admitted that to prohibit the general government, from keeping up standing armies, while yet they were authorised to raise them in case of exigency, would be an insufficient guard against the danger. A discretion of such latitude would give room to elude the force of the provision.

It is also admitted that an absolute prohibition against raising troops, except in cases of actual war, would be improper; because it will be requisite to raise and support a small number of troops to garrison the important frontier posts, and to guard arsenals; and it may happen, that the danger of an attack from a foreign power may be so imminent, as to render it highly proper we should raise an army, in order to be prepared to resist them. But to raise and keep up forces for such purposes and on such occasions, is not included in the idea, of keeping up standing armies in times of peace.

Brutus then refutes yet another argument of Hamilton:

The same writer who advances the arguments I have noticed, makes a number of other observations with a view to prove that the power to raise and keep up armies, ought to be discretionary in the general legislature; some of them are curious; he instances the raising of troops in Massachusetts and Pennsylvania, to shew the necessity of keeping a standing army in time of peace; the least reflection must convince every candid mind that both these cases are totally foreign to his purpose—Massachusetts raised a body of troops for six months, at the expiration of which they were to disband of course; this looks very little like a standing army. But beside, was that commonwealth in a state of peace at that time? So far from it that they were in the most violent commotions and contents, and their legislature had formally declared that an unnatural rebellion existed within the state. The situation of Pennsylvania was similar; a number of armed men had levied war against the authority of the state, and openly avowed their intention of withdrawing their allegiance from it. To what purpose examples are brought, of states raising troops for short periods in times of war or insurrections, on a question concerning the propriety of keeping up standing armies in times of peace, the public must judge.

Brutus also raises the subject of conscription in his discussion of the evils of standing armies. After informing his readers that the power to raise armies under the proposed constitution is "indefinite and unlimited, and authorizes the raising of forces, as well in peace as in war," he wonders whether "the clause which impowers the Congress to pass all laws which are proper and necessary, to carry this into execution, will not authorise them to impress men for the army." For "if the general legislature deem it for the general welfare to raise a body of troops, and they cannot be procured by voluntary enlistments, it seems evident, that it will be proper and necessary to effect it, that men be impressed from the militia to make up the deficiency."

The views of Brutus on the evils of standing armies were by no means novel. How quickly do Americans forget that one of the complaints of the Colonists against King George III in the Declaration of Independence was that "he has kept among us, in times of peace, Standing Armies without the consent of our legislatures." It should also be pointed out that Brutus did not merely attack the idea of a free state having a standing army, he proposed a solution to the problem of how to entrust the government with sufficient authority to provide for the cases of an enemy attack, guard arsenals, and garrison the frontier posts, while at the same time providing "a reasonable and competent security against the evil of a standing army." His solution was to add the following clause to the new constitution:

> As standing armies in time of peace are dangerous to liberty, and have often been the means of overturning the best constitutions of government, no standing army, or troops of any description whatsoever, shall be raised or kept up by the legislature, except so many as shall be necessary for guards to the arsenals of the United States, or for garrisons to such posts on the frontiers, as it shall be deemed absolutely necessary to hold, to secure the inhabitants, and facilitate the trade with the Indians: unless when the United States are threatened with an attack or invasion from some foreign power, in which case the legislature shall be authorised to raise an army to be prepared to repel the attack; provided that no troops whatsoever shall be raised in time of peace, without the assent of two thirds of the members, composing both houses of the legislature.

Brutus believed that not only would a clause like this "afford sufficient latitude to the legislature to raise troops in all cases that were really necessary," it would at the same time provide "competent security against the establishment of that dangerous engine of despotism a standing army."

The statements of Brutus on the evils of standing armies are also applicable to the current U.S. foreign policy of interventionism, for if a standing army is despotic in its own country, there is no telling how much more it may be when transplanted to a foreign country.

[All quotations from the essays of Brutus are taken from Regnery edition of The Anti-Federalists: Selected Writings and Speeches, *edited by Bruce Frohnen.]*

* * * * *

CATO ON THE EVILS OF WAR AND STANDING ARMIES

To a classical historian, Cato refers to the Roman statesmen Cato the Elder (234–139 B.C.) and Cato the Younger (95–46

B.C.). To a fashion-conscious woman, Cato is a chain of clothing stores. To a beltway libertarian, Cato refers to the Cato Institute in Washington D.C. But to the American colonists, Cato would have been a reference to the essays by John Trenchard (1662-1723) and Thomas Gordon (d. 1750) that condemned tyranny and corruption in government while advancing the principles of liberty.

Cato's Letters is a collection of 144 essays by Trenchard and Gordon that appeared in the *London Journal* and the *British Journal* between 1720 and 1723. They were published together beginning in 1724 as *Cato's Letters: Or Essays on Liberty, Civil and Religious, and Other Important Subjects*. The essays were signed with the pseudonym Cato, after Cato the Younger, the foe of Julius Caesar and champion of liberty and republican principles. Cato the Younger was the great-grandson of Cato the Elder. His daughter married Brutus, one of the assassins of Julius Caesar. Cato's life was immortalized in the 1713 play, *Cato: A Tragedy*, by the English playwright and essayist Joseph Addison (1672–1719).

Cato's Letters was not the first collaboration of Gordon and Trenchard. They also wrote and published anonymously the London political weekly, *The Independent Whig*, in 1720. Previous to this, they authored two pamphlets: *The Character of an Independent Whig* and *Considerations Offered upon the Approaching Peace and upon the Importance of Gibraltar to the British Empire, being the Second Part of the "Independent Whig,"* both published in 1719.

While *Cato's Letters* were still being published in London, they began to be reprinted in the American colonies. Thirty-seven percent of library and booksellers' catalogs surveyed in the fifty years preceding the American Revolution listed *Cato's Letters*. Trenchard and Gordon were among the ten most quoted individuals during the period from 1760–1805. According to historian Clinton Rossiter, *Cato's Letters* were "the most popular, quotable, esteemed source of political ideas in the colonial period." Bernard Bailyn further notes that to the American colonists, *Cato's Letters* "ranked with the treatises of

Locke as the most authoritative statement of the nature of political liberty."

In light of the current debacle in Iraq that the United States is engaged in, our particular concern here is the statements in *Cato's Letters* relating to the evils of war and standing armies. Although Trenchard and Gordon did not say much, they said a mouthful. Their equally notable statements on liberty and property have already been examined elsewhere.

Cato on War

The classic statement on the evils of war appears in *Cato's Letters* No. 87:

> If we consider this question under the head of justice and humanity, what can be more detestable than to murder and destroy mankind, in order to rob and pillage them? War is comprehensive of most, if not all the mischiefs which do or ever can afflict men: It depopulates nations, lays waste the finest countries, destroys arts, sciences, and learning, butchers innocents, ruins the best men, and advances the worst; effaces every trace of virtue, piety, and compassion, and introduces confusion, anarchy, and all kinds of corruption in publick affairs; and indeed is pregnant with so many evils, that it ought ever to be avoided, when it can be avoided; and it may be avoided when a state can be safe without it, and much more so when all the advantages proposed by it can be procured by prudent and just methods.

In *Cato's Letters* No. 17, as an example of "what measures have been taken by corrupt ministers, in some of our neighbouring countries, to ruin and enslave the people over whom they presided," we read something strangely reminiscent of our own "leaders":

> They will engage their country in ridiculous, expensive, fantastical wars, to keep the minds of men in continual hurry and agitation, and under constant fears and alarms;

and, by such means, deprive them both of leisure and inclination to look into publick miscarriages. Men, on the contrary, will, instead of such inspection, be disposed to fall into all measures offered, seemingly, for their defence, and will agree to every wild demand made by those who are betraying them.

When they have served their ends by such wars, or have other motives to make peace, they will have no view to the publick interest; but will often, to procure such peace, deliver up the strong-holds of their country, or its colonies for trade, to open enemies, suspected friends, or dangerous neighbours, that they may not be interrupted in their domestick designs.

This theme is continued in *Cato's Letters* No. 87:

I have often wondered at the folly and weakness of those princes, who will sacrifice hundreds of thousand of their own faithful subjects, to gain a precarious and slavish submission from bordering provinces, who will seek all opportunities to revolt; which cannot be prevented but by keeping them poor, wretched, and miserable, and consequently unable to pay the charges of their own vassalage; when, if the same number of men and the sums of money were usefully employed at home, which are necessary to make and support the conquest, they would add vastly more to their power and empire.

Cato preferred commerce to conquest:

All the advantages procured by conquest is to secure what we possess ourselves, or to gain the possessions of others, that is, the produce of their country, and the acquisitions of their labor and industry; and if these can be obtained by fair means, and by their own consent, sure it must be more eligible than to exhort them by force.

This is certainly more easily and effectually done by a well regulated commerce, than by arms: The balance of trade will return more clear money from neighbouring countries, than can be forced from them by fleets or armies, and more advantageously than under the odious name of tribute. It enervates rival states by their own consent, and obligates them, whilst it impoverishes and ruins them: It keeps our own people at home employed in arts, manufactures, and husbandry, instead of murdering them in wild, expensive, and hazardous expeditions, to the weakening their own country, and the pillaging and destroying their neighbours, and only for the fruitless and imaginary glory of conquest.

Cato on Standing Armies

Like the American Brutus, Cato also spoke out against the evils of standing armies. This subject was a particular concern of John Trenchard. With Walter Moyle, Trenchard had previously written *An Argument Shewing that a Standing Army is Inconsistent with a Free Government, and Absolutely Destructive to the Constitution of the English Monarchy* (London, 1697). This was followed the next year by Trenchard's *A Short History of Standing Armies in England* (London, 1698). He was also the author of the anonymously-published work, *A Letter from the Author of the Argument Against a Standing Army, to the Author of the Ballancing Letter* [an essay defending standing armies] (London, 1697).

Cato's Letters No. 94 and 95 are both devoted to the subject of standing armies. The subject is also mentioned in another essay entitled "Considerations upon the Condition of an Absolute Prince." Sometimes it is standing armies in general that are warned against:

Standing armies are standing curses in every country under the sun, where they are more powerful than the people.

It is certain, that all parts of Europe which are enslaved, have been enslaved by armies; and it is absolutely impossible, that any nation which keeps them amongst themselves can long preserve their liberties; nor can any nation perfectly lose their liberties who are without such guests: And yet, though all men see this, and at times confess it, yet all have joined in their turns, to bring this heavy evil upon themselves and their country.

I never yet met with one honest and reasonable man out of power who was not heartily against all standing armies, as threatening and pernicious, and the ready instruments of certain ruin: And I scarce ever met with a man in power, or even the meanest creature of power, who was not for defending and keeping them up: So much are the opinions of men guided by their circumstances! Men, when they are angry with one another, will come into any measures for revenge, without considering that the same power which destroys an enemy, may destroy themselves; and he to whom I lend my sword to kill my foe, may with it kill me.

Great empires cannot subsist without great armies, and liberty cannot subsist with them. As armies long kept up, and grown part of the government, will soon engross the whole government, and can never be disbanded; so liberty long lost, can never be recovered. Is not this an awful lesson to free states, to be vigilant against a dreadful condition, which has no remedy.

At other times the reference is specific and contemporary:

When, in King William's reign, the question was in debate, Whether England should be ruled by standing armies? The argument commonly used by some, who had the presumption to call themselves Whigs, and owned in the Ballancing Letter (supposed to be written by one who gave the word to all the rest), was, that all governments must have their periods one time or other, and when that time came, all endeavours to preserve liberty were fruitless; and shrewd hints were given in that letter, that England was reduced to such a condition; that our corruptions were so great, and the dissatisfaction of the people was so general, that the publick safety could not be preserved, but by increasing the power of the crown: And this argument was used by those shameless men, who had caused all that corruption, and all that dissatisfaction.

I should be glad to know in what situation of our affairs it can be safe to reduce our troops to the usual guards and garrisons, if it cannot be done now. There is no power in Europe considerable enough to threaten us, who can have any motives to do so, if we pursue the old maxims and natural interest of Great Britain; which is, to meddle no farther with foreign squabbles, than to keep the balance even between France and Spain.

And once again it is commerce that "saves the trouble, expence, and hazard, of supporting numerous standing armies abroad to keep the conquered people in subjection; armies, who, for the most part too, if not always, enslave their own country, and ever swallow up all the advantages of the conquests."

The current U.S. policies of militarism and interventionism are directly contrary to the wisdom of Trenchard and Gordon in *Cato's Letters*. If the Founding Fathers considered these essays to be so important, why doesn't Bush and Company think likewise?

[All quotations from Cato's Letters *are taken from the Liberty Fund edition edited by Ronald Hamowy, which is also available online.]*

* * * * *

Jefferson on the Evils of War

The Jeffersonian principles of peace, commerce, honest friendship with all nations, and entangling alliances with none, as annunciated in Jefferson's First Inaugural Address, are no where more evident than in his opinion of war.

War and Peace

Jefferson was a man of peace. President Polk will ever be

associated with the Mexican War, Lincoln with the Civil War, McKinley with the Spanish-American War, Wilson with World War I, Roosevelt with World War II, Johnson with Vietnam, Bush I with Gulf War I, and Bush II with the ongoing debacle in Iraq. But such is not the case with Jefferson. Even though he is usually considered to be one of the "great" presidents, he is not remembered as such because he was associated with a major war.

As a man of peace, he often made a contrast between the blessings of peace and the scourge of war:

> I love peace, and am anxious that we should give the world still another useful lesson, by showing to them other modes of punishing injuries than by war, which is as much a punishment to the punisher as to the sufferer.

> War has been avoided from a due sense of the miseries, and the demoralization it produces, and of the superior blessings of a state of peace and friendship with all mankind.

> I value peace, and I should unwillingly see any event take place which would render war a necessary resource.

> Having seen the people of all other nations bowed down to the earth under the wars and prodigalities of their rulers, I have cherished their opposites, peace, economy, and riddance of public debt, believing that these were the high road to public as well as private prosperity and happiness.

> Believing that the happiness of mankind is best promoted by the useful pursuits of peace, that on these alone a stable prosperity can be founded, that the evils of war are great in their endurance, and have a long reckoning for ages to come, I have used my best endeavors to keep our country uncommitted in the troubles which afflict Europe, and which assail us on every side.

> I do not believe war the most certain means of enforcing principles. Those peaceable coercions which are in the power of every nation, if undertaken in concert and in time of peace, are more likely to produce the desired effect.

We love and we value peace; we know its blessings from experience. We abhor the follies of war, and are not untried in its distresses and calamities.

On several occasions, Jefferson presented his philosophy of peace to some Indian tribes:

The evils which of necessity encompass the life of man are sufficiently numerous. Why should we add to them by voluntarily distressing and destroying one another? Peace, brothers, is better than war. In a long and bloody war, we lose many friends, and gain nothing. Let us then live in peace and friendship together, doing to each other all the good we can.

Born in the same land, we ought to live as brothers, doing to each other all the good we can, and not listening to wicked men, who may endeavor to make us enemies. By living in peace, we can help and prosper one another; by waging war, we can kill and destroy many on both sides; but those who survive will not be the happier for that.

How much better is it for neighbours to help than to hurt one another. How much happier must it make them. If you will cease to make war on one another, if you will live in friendship with all mankind, you can employ all your time in providing food and clothing for yourselves and your families; your men will not be destroyed in war; and your women and children will lie down to sleep in their cabins without fear of being surprised by their enemies and killed or carried away. Your numbers will be increased instead of diminishing, and you will live in plenty and in quiet.

The Evils of War

Because Jefferson was a man of peace, he considered war to be a great evil:

I abhor war and view it as the greatest scourge of mankind.

The insults & injuries committed on us by both the belligerent parties, from the beginning of 1793 to this day, & still continuing, cannot now be wiped off by engaging in war with one of them.

I have seen enough of one war never to wish to see another.

One war, such as that of our Revolution, is enough for one life.

The most successful war seldom pays for its losses.

War is as much a punishment to the punisher as to the sufferer.

War is an instrument entirely inefficient toward redressing wrong; and multiplies, instead of indemnifying losses.

We have obtained by a peaceable appeal to justice, in four months, what we should not have obtained under seven years of war, the loss of one hundred thousand lives, an hundred millions of additional debt, many hundred millions worth of produce and property lost for want of market, or in seeking it, and that demoralization which war superinduces on the human mind.

Great sacrifices of interest have certainly been made by our nation under the difficulties latterly forced upon us by transatlantic powers. But every candid and reflecting mind must agree with you, that while these were temporary and bloodless, they were calculated to avoid permanent subjection to foreign law and tribute, relinquishment of independent rights, and the burthens, the havoc, and desolations of war.

War and the Nations

Jefferson did not consider a nation to be great because of its military might: "Wars and contentions, indeed, fill the pages of history with more matter. But more blessed is that nation whose silent course of happiness furnishes nothing for history to say." He considered war between nations to be "the consequence of a want of respectability in the national character." Regarding the attitude toward war of the people of the United States, Jefferson believed that "no country, perhaps, was ever so thoroughly against war as ours. These dispositions pervade every description of its citizens, whether in or out of office."

He knew firsthand the folly of getting involved in European wars:

> Wars with any European powers are devoutly to be deprecated.

> For years we have been looking as spectators on our brethren in Europe, afflicted by all those evils which necessarily follow an abandonment of the moral rules which bind men and nations together. Connected with them in friendship and commerce, we have happily so far kept aloof from their calamitous conflicts, by a steady observance of justice towards all, by much forbearance and multiplied sacrifices. At length, however, all regard to the rights of others having been thrown aside, the belligerent powers have beset the highway of commercial intercourse with edicts which, taken together, expose our commerce and mariners, under almost every destination, a prey to their fleets and armies. Each party, indeed, would admit our commerce with themselves, with the view of associating us in their war against the other. But we have wished war with neither.

> It is much to be desired that war may be avoided, if circumstances will admit. Nor in the present maniac state of Europe, should I estimate the point of honor by the ordinary scale. I believe we shall on the contrary, have credit with the world, for having made the avoidance of being engaged in the present unexampled war, our first object.

> The cannibals of Europe are going to eating one another again. A war between Russia and Turkey is like the battle of the kite and snake. Whichever destroys the other, leaves a

destroyer the less for the world. This pugnacious humor of mankind seems to be the law of his nature, one of the obstacles to too great multiplication provided in the mechanism of the Universe. The cocks of the henyard kill one another up. Bears, bulls, rams, do the same. And the horse, in his wild state, kills all the young males, until worn down with age and war, some vigorous youth kills him, and takes to himself the harem of females. I hope we shall prove how much happier for man the Quaker policy is, and that the life of the feeder is better than that of the fighter; and it is some consolation that the desolation by these maniacs of one part of the earth is the means of improving it in other parts. Let the latter be our office, and let us milk the cow, while the Russian holds her by the horns, and the Turk by the tail.

He recognized that geography was one of the great advantages of the United States: "The insulated state in which nature has placed the American continent should so far avail it that no spark of war kindled in the other quarters of the globe should be wafted across the wide oceans which separate us from them." With a very few exceptions, the United States has always had to cross oceans to wage its wars.

Jefferson realized that the push for war comes, not from the people in the nations, but from the governments of the nations:

We have received a report that the French Directory has proposed a declaration of war against the United States to the Council of Ancients, who have rejected it. Thus we see two nations, who love one another affectionately, brought by the ill temper of their executive administrations, to the very brink of a necessity to imbrue their hands in the blood of each other.

The agents of the two people [United States and France] are either great bunglers or great rascals, when they cannot preserve that peace which is the universal wish of both.

The people now see that France has sincerely wished peace, and their seducers [federalists] have wished war, as well for

the loaves and fishes which arise out of war expenses, as for
the chance of changing the Constitution, while the people
should have time to contemplate nothing but the levies of
men and money.

No one wakes up in the morning with the desire to drop bombs
on people in foreign countries that he does not know, have
never injured him in any way, and are no threat to him or his
family. This desire is always government induced and government sponsored. When it comes to mass murder, the state takes
a backseat to no one.

Jefferson thought it beneficial for a nation to avoid war:

Never was so much false arithmetic employed on any
subject, as that which has been employed to persuade
nations that it is their interest to go to war. Were the
money which it has cost to gain, at the close of a long war,
a little town, or a little territory, the right to cut wood here,
or to catch fish there, expended in improving what they
already possess, in making roads, opening rivers, building
ports, improving the arts, and finding employment for their
idle poor, it would render them much stronger, much
wealthier and happier. This I hope will be our wisdom.

Jefferson believed that the best policy for the United States
toward other nations was one of friendship and nonintervention:

Unmeddling with the affairs of other nations, we had hoped
that our distance and our dispositions would have left us
free, in the example and indulgence of peace with all the
world.

To cherish and maintain the rights and liberties of our
citizens, and to ward from them the burthens, the miseries,
and the crimes of war, by a just and friendly conduct
toward all nations, were among the most obvious and
important duties of those to whom the management of their
public interests have been confided; and happy shall we be

if a conduct guided by these views on our part, shall secure to us a reciprocation of peace and justice from other nations.

The desire to preserve our country from the calamities and ravages of war, by cultivating a disposition, and pursuing a conduct, conciliatory and friendly to all nations, has been sincerely entertained and faithfully followed.

He much preferred commerce to war: "War is not the best engine for us to resort to; nature has given us one in our commerce, which, if properly managed, will be a better instrument for obliging the interested nations of Europe to treat us with justice." The current U.S. foreign policy of belligerency, intervention, hegemony, and subjugation is a far cry from the example of Jefferson.

The Advent of War

It is true that Jefferson did believe in war under certain circumstances:

If ever there was a holy war, it was that which saved our liberties and gave us independence.

It is our duty still to endeavor to avoid war; but if it shall actually take place, no matter by whom brought on, we must defend ourselves. If our house be on fire, without inquiring whether it was fired from within or without, we must try to extinguish it. In that, I have no doubt, we shall act as one man.

Obviously, traversing oceans to bomb places that many Americans cannot even locate on a map would not fall into this category.

But even though Jefferson realized that war might take place, he had his doubts as to whether we would be better off at its conclusion: "If we are forced into war [with France], we must give up political differences of opinion, and unite as one man to defend our country. But whether at the close of such a war, we should be as free as we are now, God knows." If a war was necessary then it should not be undertaken "till our revenue shall be entirely liberated from debt. Then it will suffice for war, without creating new debt or taxes." But Jefferson opposed "taxing the industry of our fellow citizens to accumulate treasure for wars to happen we know not when and which might not perhaps happen but from the temptations offered by that treasure."

He also did not believe in the bloodthirsty doctrine of "total war" that the United States has engaged in since 1862. In a model treaty drawn up while he was in France, Jefferson contended that if contracting parties went to war, their trade should not be interrupted, prisoners were to be given good treatment, merchants were to be given time to settle their affairs and depart peacefully from enemy territory, and women, children, and scholars were to be considered non-combatants. (It is inconceivable that Jefferson, or any of the Founding Fathers, could ever have considered women serving in combat or semi-combat roles à la Jessica Lynch.)

On actually abolishing war, Jefferson was certainly no utopian, and stated: "I hope it is practicable, by improving the mind and morals of society, to lessen the disposition to war; but of its abolition I despair."

The Declaration of War

Jefferson was particularly concerned about the executive branch of government having the war power. Our modern Jeffersonian in Congress, Rep. Ron Paul (R-TX), was one of the few legislators to voice similar concerns as the U.S. was poised to invade Iraq. Here again is Jefferson:

> The power of declaring war being with the Legislature, the Executive should do nothing necessarily committing them to decide for war in preference of non-intercourse, which will be preferred by a great many.

I opposed the right of the President to declare anything future on the question, Shall there or shall there not be war?

Considering that Congress alone is constitutionally invested with the power of changing our condition from peace to war, I have thought it my duty to await their authority for using force in any degree which could be avoided. I have barely instructed the officers stationed in the neighborhood of the aggressions to protect our citizens from violence, to patrol within the borders actually delivered to us, and not to go out of them but when necessary to repel an inroad or to rescue a citizen or his property.

As the Executive cannot decide the question of war on the affirmative side, neither ought it to do so on the negative side, by preventing the competent body from deliberating on the question.

Congress [must] be called [if there] is a justifiable cause of war; and as the Executive cannot decide the question of war on the affirmative side, neither ought it to do so on the negative side by preventing the competent body from deliberating on the question.

We have already given in example one effectual check to the Dog of war by transferring the power of letting him loose from the Executive to the Legislative body, from those who are to spend to those who are to pay.

The making reprisal on a nation is a very serious thing. Remonstrance and refusal of satisfaction ought to precede; and when reprisal follows, it is considered as an act of war, and never yet failed to produce it in the case of a nation able to make war; besides, if the case were important enough to require reprisal, and ripe for that step, Congress must be called on to take it; the right of reprisal being expressly lodged with them by the Constitution, and not with the Executive.

The question of war being placed by the Constitution with

the Legislature alone, respect to that [makes] it [the Executive's] duty to restrain the operations of our militia to those merely defensive; and considerations involving the public satisfaction, and peculiarly my own, require that the decision of that question, whichever way it be, should be pronounced definitely by the Legislature themselves.

Standing Armies

Like the British Cato and the American Brutus, Jefferson was averse to standing armies:

There are instruments so dangerous to the rights of the nation and which place them so totally at the mercy of their governors that those governors, whether legislative or executive, should be restrained from keeping such instruments on foot but in well-defined cases. Such an instrument is a standing army.

Were armies to be raised whenever a speck of war is visible in our horizon, we never should have been without them. Our resources would have been exhausted on dangers which have never happened, instead of being reserved for what is really to take place.

Nor is it conceived needful or safe that a standing army should be kept up in time of peace.

The spirit of this country is totally adverse to a large military force.

In another statement regarding relations with the Indians, Jefferson again decried standing armies:

We must do as the Spaniards and English do. Keep them in peace by liberal and constant presents. Another powerful motive is that in this way we may leave no pretext for raising or continuing an army. Every rag of an Indian depredation will, otherwise, serve as a ground to raise troops with those who think a standing army and a public debt necessary for the happiness of the United States, and we shall never be permitted to get rid of either.

Conclusion

Jefferson was not alone in his views on the evils of war. Most of the Founding Fathers thought likewise:

"Of all the enemies to public liberty, war is perhaps the most to be dreaded because it comprises and develops the germ of every other." ~ James Madison

"There was never a good war or a bad peace." ~ Benjamin Franklin

"Preparation for war is a constant stimulus to suspicion and ill will." ~ James Monroe

"While there are knaves and fools in the world, there will be wars in it." ~ John Jay

"The fiery and destructive passions of war reign in the human breast with much more powerful sway than the mild and beneficent sentiments of peace." ~ Alexander Hamilton

"My first wish is to see this plague of mankind, war, banished from the earth." ~ George Washington

But today, instead of sages like Madison, Franklin, Monroe, Jay, Hamilton, Washington, and Jefferson, we have warmongers like Bush, Cheney, Libby, Feith, Wolfowitz, Rumsfeld, Perle, and Abrams. And instead of the wisdom of the Founding Fathers, the American public is fed a steady diet of David Frum, William Kristol, Sean Hannity, Jonah Goldberg, Max Boot, Fox News, and the *War Street Journal*.

Jefferson was not perfect, and he was at times inconsistent, but overall his principles were sound. The senseless waste of American lives in Bush's Iraq fiasco could have been avoided if

Jefferson's aversion to war had been followed instead of forsaken, as have the other sound principles of the Founders.

[These quotations from Jefferson have been taken from a variety of sources. Most are from the now out-of-print volume, The Complete Jefferson, *edited and assembled by Saul K. Padover. However, other similar volumes of Jefferson's writings are available, and much is now available online, such as this collection of Jefferson's letters.]*

* * * * *

EIGHT FACTS ABOUT IRAQ

The Bush administration, its accomplices in the news media, and the conservative talk show hacks who do the bidding of the Republican party have sold America a bill of goods. The invasion of Iraq was justified, we have been led to believe, because Saddam Hussein was the reincarnation of Adolph Hitler, Iraq was in the position of Germany on the eve of World War II, and the "elite" Republican Guard was the equivalent of the German Wehrmacht. According to the president himself: "We will end a brutal regime, whose aggression and weapons of mass destruction make it a unique threat to the world."

Right wing Christians too, who ought to know better, have also been duped because of their misplaced trust in the state just because it is currently controlled by the Republican party (the same Republican party that is expanding government at a rate not seen since the Democratic administrations of Lyndon Johnson and Franklin Roosevelt).

Located at the northern tip of the Persian Gulf, and encompassing the land of ancient Mesopotamia, as well as the biblical Tigris and Euphrates rivers, the country of Iraq, which until recently could not be located on a map by most Americans, is now the focus of all Americans. But because most Americans are woefully ignorant of history, and especially the history of U.S. intervention into other countries; and because most Christians are just as ignorant of history, and especially Christians who spend all their time believing what they read in the newspaper, hear on the radio, and see on television, some facts about Iraq are in order.

Fact Number 1: *There was no country of Iraq until it was created by the British in 1920.* In 1534 the Ottoman Turks conquered the area of what is now Iraq. Here the Ottoman empire ruled until its defeat in World War I because Turkey sided with the Central powers. After World War I, the French and British divided up the formerly Ottoman-controlled lands in the Middle East. France was given a League of Nations mandate over Syria and Lebanon; Great Britain was given the same over

Palestine, Transjordan, and Iraq. The modern state of Iraq was created out of the three Ottoman provinces of Basra, Mosul, and Baghdad. The defeat of the Turks may have brought to an end the Ottoman empire, but it began a century of Western imperialism.

Fact Number 2: *The United States already sponsored two previous regime changes in Iraq.* Under their League of Nations mandate, the British installed King Faisal as the ruler of Iraq. But even after its independence, Iraq was still controlled by Britain. Faisal's dynasty lasted until his grandson Faisal II was executed in a 1958 coup. The Hitler in Iraq in the early 1960s was Abd al-Karim Qasim. After deposing the Western-allied Iraqi monarchy in 1958, Qasim was seen by the U.S. as a counter to Gamal Abdel Nassar of Egypt. But after he was perceived as too much of a threat to Western oil interests, Qasim was killed in February 1963 in a CIA-sponsored coup by the anti-Communist Baath party. American firms soon began doing business with Baghdad. All was not well, however, in the Baath party, for in 1968 an internal coup brought to power General Ahmad Hassan al-Bakr, who was succeeded by Saddam Hussein in 1979. These regime changes in Iraq were both accompanied by bloody reprisals.

Fact Number 3: *Saddam Hussein was an ally of the United States until the first Persian Gulf War.* The U.S.–Hussein connection actually goes all the way back to the late 1950s. Hussein was part of a group that tried to assassinate Abd al-Karim Qasim after he seized power in 1958. Fleeing Iraq, he eventually settled in Cairo, Egypt, where he was courted by the CIA. During the 1980s, when Iraq was at war with Iran, military intelligence was provided to Iraq because the United States sought to do whatever was necessary to prevent Iraq from losing its war with Iran. The U.S. problem with Iran stemmed from decades of American intervention that backfired when radical Shiite Muslims overthrew the Shah and installed the Ayatollah Khomeini. The United States has a bad habit of collaborating with tyrants who later come back to bite us. Who can forget that Joseph Stalin, one of the bloodiest killers who ever lived, was our "ally" in World War II?

Fact Number 4: *Iraq got its "weapons of mass destruction" from the United States.* This started after the Baath party coup of 1963, when the U.S. sent arms to the new regime. But during the Iran–Iraq War of the 1980s, when, under the successive administrations of Reagan and Bush I, Saddam Hussein was our ally against Iran, it was not just arms that were provided to Iraq. According to the 1992 U.S. Senate committee report on U.S. Chemical and Biological Warfare-Related Dual-Use Exports to Iraq, "The United States provided the government of Iraq with 'dual use' licensed materials which assisted in the development of Iraqi chemical, biological and missile-system programs." This included anthrax, VX nerve gas, West Nile fever germs, botulism, salmonella, and E coli.

Fact Number 5: *Iraq was a liberal Muslim state.* Iraq is made up of three major groups: the Kurds, the Shiites, and the Sunnis. The Shiites, which are in the majority, are the more radical Muslims. The ruling Baath party was more closely associated with the more moderate Sunnis, which make up about 35 percent of the population. Unlike Saudi Arabia, Iran, and most other Muslim states, Iraq was not controlled by a fundamentalist Muslim government, something that is now a possibility. One could even purchase a drink in Baghdad. The Baath government tolerated both Jews and Christians, something not to be seen in Muslim countries like Indonesia, Turkey, and Iran.

Fact Number 6: *Iraq was not responsible for the 9-11 attacks on the United States.* Many Americans who supported the war with Iraq did so because they were led to believe that the U.S. was retaliating for the terrorist attacks on September 11. Yet, none of the hijackers of the airplanes on September 11 were from Iraq (or Afghanistan). They were mainly from Saudi Arabia, our supposed Muslim ally in the Middle East. No connection has ever been proved between Iraq and al-Qaeda or Saddam Hussein and Osama bin Laden. There is even evidence that the invasion of Iraq was planned before the September 11 attacks. A September 2000 document issued by the Project for the New American Century (PNAC) entitled "Rebuilding

America's Defenses: Strategies, Forces and Resources For A New Century," drawn up by Dick Cheney, Donald Rumsfeld, and Paul Wolfowitz, shows that Bush's cabinet intended to take military control of the Persian Gulf region regardless of whether Saddam Hussein was in power.

Fact Number 7: *Iraq was not a threat to the United States.* Although Bush's initial justification for war was that Iraq was a "threat to the United Nations" (certainly no reason for the U.S. to go to war), this was soon shifted to Iraq being a threat to the United States. But even though Secretary of Defense Donald Rumsfeld insisted that "no terrorist state poses a greater and more immediate threat to the security of our people and the stability of the world than the regime of Saddam Hussein in Iraq," the condition of Iraq said otherwise. Not only was Iraq's army considerably weaker than it was during the first Persian Gulf War—a war in which Iraq only managed to kill 148 Americans—but Iraq had no navy or air force. Iraq's economy was in ruin after a decade of sanctions—sanctions that destroyed its water supplies. The GNP of Iraq was not even 15 percent of that of the state of Washington. The only time in history when Iraq did actually attack the United States—an Iraqi warplane attacked a U.S. ship in the Persian Gulf in 1987 resulting in the killing of dozens of U.S. sailors—we did nothing because Iraq apologized for its "mistake." No, the greatest threat to freedoms of the American people is not Iraq. The greatest threat to the freedoms of the American people is not some country six thousand miles away; it is our own government. How is it that in a country with such a heritage of individual liberty like the United States, one can smoke in a restaurant in Baghdad, but not in Manhattan? How is it that in a country with a Christian heritage like the United States, one can buy a gun in Baghdad, but not in Washington D. C.? If Iraq's neighboring countries did not feel the need to send troops to Baghdad, then why did we?

Fact Number 8: *Iraq is the Mideast's second largest oil producer.* Although this is a fact that everyone knows, it is downplayed by all proponents of the war with Iraq. But if oil has nothing to do with the U.S. intervening in Iraq, then why hasn't the U.S. intervened in Sudan, where 2 million Christians have been killed during the past decade? What about the persecution of Christians in Indonesia? Why hasn't the U.S. intervened in Zimbabwe, where the Marxist tyrant Robert Mugabe has been confiscating the country's farmland? Why has Fidel Castro—90 miles away from our shores—been untouched for 40 years? Why didn't the U.S. instigate a "regime change" when Idi Amin was killing thousands of his own black people in Uganda in the 1970s? Why didn't the U.S. instigate a "regime change" when the Tutsis were slaughtered by the Hutu government of Rwanda in 1994? Would things have been different if Sudan, Indonesia, Zimbabwe, Cuba, Uganda, and Rwanda had significant oil reserves?

These sobering facts, unknown to Americans who get all their news from ABC, CBS, NBC, CNN, FOX, and CNBC, should cause every citizen, and especially every Christian, to question the motives of the state the next time it is insisted that we should invade another country. They should also cause all Americans to question the necessity of the United States maintaining 184 military bases in over 100 countries around the world. God never appointed the United States to be the world's policeman.

* * * * *

THE WAR TO END ALL WARS

One hundred and fifty years ago, France and Great Britain intervened in what was, and should have remained, a dispute between Russia and Turkey. The official beginning of what came to be called the Crimean War was on March 28, 1854, when Great Britain and France declared war on Russia. Coming between Napoleon's defeat at Waterloo in 1815 and the beginning of World War I in 1914, the Crimean War should have been the "war to end all wars" instead of being a precursor to the carnage of the war that made "the world safe for democracy."

There are three things that came out of the Crimean War that most people are familiar with but have no idea that they are connected with it: the nurse Florence Nightingale, the poem "The Charge of the Light Brigade," and the novel *War and Peace*.

Florence Nightingale (1820–1910) was the famed pioneer of nursing and reformer of hospital sanitation methods. After hearing of the deplorable conditions that existed in the British Military Hospital at Scutari, opposite of Constantinople, she arrived in the Crimea with 38 nurses on November 4, 1854, and soon began to improve the conditions at the hospital.

"The Charge of the Light Brigade" was the poem written by Alfred Lord Tennyson (1809–1892) that immortalized the disastrous British cavalry charge which occurred during the Crimean War at the Battle of Balaclava on October 25, 1854.

> "Forward, the Light Brigade!"
> Was there a man dismay'd?
> Not tho' the soldiers knew
> Some one had blunder'd:
> Their's not to make reply
> Their's not to reason why,
> Their's but to do and die:
> Into the valley of Death
> Rode the Six Hundred.

Set in Russia during the Napoleonic Era, *War and Peace*, by the Russian writer Leo Tolstoy (1828–1910), is the epic novel published between 1865 and 1869. Although most people have never read it, because it contains 365 chapters, *War and Peace* is the book usually mentioned when one wants to compare some daunting task to reading an unusually large book. The connection between *War and Peace* and the Crimean War? Tolstoy was a Russian second lieutenant in the Crimean War, and therefore an eyewitness to battle scenes he so realistically describes in this novel.

Located in southern Ukraine, the Crimean peninsula juts into the Black Sea and connects to the mainland by the Isthmus of Perekop. Its area is about 9,700 square miles. Dry steppes, scattered with numerous burial-mounds of the ancient Scythians, cover more than two-thirds of the peninsula, with the Crimean mountains in the south rising to heights of 5,000 ft. before dropping sharply to the Black Sea.

Various peoples have occupied the Crimean peninsula over the years: Goths, Huns, Scythians, Khazars, Greeks, Kipchaks, Mongols. The Ottoman Turks conquered the region in 1475. In 1783, the whole of the Crimea was annexed to the Russian Empire. The Crimea was the scene of some bloody battles in the Second World War. It was also the site of the "Big Three" (Roosevelt, Churchill, and Stalin) Conference held in the former palace of Czar Nicholas at Yalta, a city on the Crimean south-eastern shore of the Black Sea. It was here during the week of February 4–11, 1945, that Roosevelt delivered Eastern Europe to Stalin.

The underlying cause of the Crimean War was the Eastern Question—the international problem of European territory controlled by the decaying Ottoman Empire. The immediate causes of the Crimean War were religious. Now, there is nothing the least bit "religious" about war, but, without a complete separation of church and state, religion is often used by the state as a pretext for war. Russia (Orthodox) was engaged in a dispute with France (Catholic) over the guardianship of the "Holy Places" in Palestine, and a dispute with the Ottoman Turks over the protection of the Orthodox Christians subject to the Ottoman sultan. Russia demanded from the Turks that there be established a Russian protectorate over all Orthodox subjects in the Ottoman Empire. After Turkey refused, Russia, in July of 1853, occupied the Ottoman vassal states of Moldavia and Walachia. The czar made the claim that "by the occupation of the Principalities we desire such security as will ensure the restoration of our dues. It is not conquest that we seek but satisfaction for a just right so clearly infringed."

In October of the same year, the Ottoman Turks declared war on Russia. War between Russia and Turkey was nothing new, as the Russo-Turkish Wars (1768–74, 1787–92, 1828–29) evidence. They had first clashed over Astrakhan in 1569. Although Constantinople had fallen to the Turks in 1453, the Ottoman Empire was in decline, and Russia, since the time of Peter the Great (1672–1725), had wanted to secure a warm-water outlet to the Mediterranean—at the expense of Ottoman territory. This naturally upset France and Great Britain, which saw Russian ambitions as a threat to the balance of power in the Mediterranean. Russia was given an ultimatum demanding the withdrawal of its forces from the principalities. When Russia refused, France and Great Britain, having already dispatched fleets to the Black Sea, declared war on Russia on March 28, 1854. The Anglo-Franco alliance was a precarious one. France and Great Britain had historically been enemies, but, like Herod and Pilate, who "were made friends together" when they allied to condemn Christ (Luke 23:1–12), they united to check the ambitions of Russia, under the guise of defending Turkey.

Most of the subsequent fighting took place in the Crimea because of the strategic Russian naval base at Sevastopol on the southwestern coast. The accession of a new czar in Russia (Alexander II) and the capture of Sevastopol led to the Treaty of Paris (March 30, 1856) that ended the war and the dominant role of Russia in Southeast Europe. Britain and France saved the Ottoman empire, an empire that they would help destroy in World War I.

The Crimean War is known for a number of "firsts": deadly-accurate rifles, significant use of the telegraph, tactical use of railways, life-saving medical innovations, trench combat, undersea mines, "live" reporting to newspapers, and cigarettes.

But there is one other thing that began with the Crimean War that should have made it the war to end all wars: photography.

Although photography had only recently been invented before the Crimean War, it had progressed enough so as to make it possible to photograph the horrors of war. The wet collodion process by Frederick Scott Archer (1813–1857), introduced in 1850, cut exposure times from minutes to seconds.

War correspondents Thomas Chenery and William Russell

relayed some of the horrors of war back to *The Times* in Britain. Thomas Agnew, of the publishing house Thomas Agnew & Sons, then proposed sending a photographer to the Crimea as a strictly private, commercial venture. The British government had previously made several official attempts to document the war with photographs. One effort ended in shipwreck, and none of the photographs survive from the other two.

Enter Roger Fenton (1819–1869). Fenton, who had previously photographed the royal family, spent four months in the Crimea (March 8 to June 26, 1855) photographing the war. He had the cooperation of Prince Albert and the ministry of war, as well as the field commanders in the Crimea. After converting a horse-drawn wine merchant's "van" into a mobile darkroom, Fenton, his assistants, horses, photographic van, and equipment were transported to the Crimea courtesy of the British government. He returned to Britain with 360 photographs and cholera.

On September 20th, 1855, an exhibit of 312 of the photographs opened in London. Sets of photographs went on sale in November. Although the pictures were widely reviewed and advertised, when the war ended, interest in photographs of the war ended with it, and the entire stock of unsold prints and negatives were auctioned off by December of 1856. Fenton abandoned photography in 1862, putting an advertisement in the *Photographic Journal* to dispose of his equipment.

In 1944, the Library of Congress purchased 263 of Fenton's prints from one of his relatives. The Roger Fenton Crimean War photographs, thought to be Fenton's proof prints made upon his return, can be viewed online and freely downloaded, including his most well-known photograph, "Valley of the Shadow of Death."

While Fenton's photographs show plenty of scenes of military supplies, camp life, groups of soldiers, the leading figures of the allied armies, and landscape scenes, there are no scenes of combat or devastation. He wrote about scenes of death and destruction that he witnessed, but he did not photograph any of them. At the scene of the Light Brigade's ill-fated charge, he saw "skeletons half-buried, one was lying as if he had raised himself upon his elbow, the bare skull sticking up with still enough flesh in the muscles to prevent it falling from the shoulders." But whether it was because of an explicit directive from, or an implicit understanding with, the British government, the fact remains that Fenton witnessed the horrors of war, and had ample opportunity to photograph them, but didn't. For political or commercial reasons, or both, the war was portrayed in the best possible light. A positive report was needed to counter negative press reports and to encourage the British nation to support the war effort. For this reason, Fenton's photographs can be considered the first instance of photographic propaganda.

The Crimean War destroyed the lives of over 200,000 men. How many Russians could have become another Boris Pasternak or Igor Sikorsky? How many British could have become another Christopher Wren or Isaac Newton? How many French could have become another Victor Hugo or Frédéric Bastiat? How many Turks could have become another Mustafa Kemal or Ali Erdemir. God only knows. The Crimean War could have and should have been the war to end all wars. Instead, as A. N. Wilson remarks in *The Victorians*, it was the greatest blunder of the nineteenth century, setting up animosities and alliances that led to World War I and the continuing turmoil of Eastern Europe, the Middle East, and Central Asia.

[For the latest book on the Crimean War, see Trevor Royle's Crimea: The Great Crimean War 1854-1856.]

* * * * *

THE HORRORS OF WAR

"It is well that war is so terrible, lest we grow too fond of it." ~ Robert E. Lee

"The evils of war are great in their endurance, and have a long reckoning for ages to come." ~ Thomas Jefferson

Current Conflicts

At the dawning of the year 2004, there were fifteen major wars in progress, plus twenty more "lesser" conflicts. According to Global Security, there are now conflicts raging in the following places:

Afghanistan (Taliban and Al Qaida)
Algeria (insurgency by Muslim fundamentalists)
Angola (secessionist conflict in Angola's Cabinda enclave)
Burma (insurgency by ethnic minority groups)
Burundi (civil war between ethnic groups)
China (dispute with other countries over ownership of Spratly Islands)
Colombia (insurgency by various guerilla groups)
Democratic Republic of the Congo (Congo War involving nine African nations)
Georgia (conflict with Russia, ethnic group conflict)
India (longstanding conflicts in Assam and Kashmir; Naxalite uprising)
Indonesia (conflicts in Aceh, Kalimantan, Maluku, and Papua)
Iraq (occupation by U.S. forces)
Israel (Intifada)
Ivory Coast (civil war)
Liberia (ritual killings and cannibalism)
Moldova (Transdniester independence movement)
Namibia (Caprivi Strip liberation movement)
Nepal (Maoist insurgency)
Nigeria (religious and ethnic conflicts)
Peru (Shining Path terrorist movement)
Philippines (Moro Islamic Liberation Front uprising)
Russia (Chechen uprising)
Somalia (civil war)
Spain (Basque uprising)
Sri Lanka (Tamil uprising)
Sudan (civil war)
Thailand (Islamic insurgency)
Turkey (Kurdish separatist movement)
Uganda (civil unrest)

Although the United Nations was founded "to save succeeding generations from the scourge of war, which twice in our lifetime has brought untold sorrow to mankind," there have been more conflicts in the world since the founding of the UN than during any previous period in history.

The United States maintains a global empire of troops and bases that would make a Roman emperor look like the mayor of a small town.

War

Too much has been written throughout history that glorifies war and the warrior who is sent by the state to do its bidding. Dying for one's country—regardless of the circumstances that brought on the conflict—is seen as the ultimate sacrifice. To protest the war is to be a traitor. Being a professional soldier is viewed as one of the noblest of occupations. The death of enemy combatants is celebrated. Civilian casualties are written off as "collateral damage."

In the current Iraq war, before the phoney transfer of power on June 28, 855 American troops had died. That is 800 young men (and women) who will never gave their parents any grandchildren or who left behind grieving wives and children. Forgotten are the over 5000 military personnel who were injured, many of whom will endure suffering the rest of their life. And that number is just the "official" figure. The thousands of Iraqi troops killed or injured are not much of a concern to anyone—and neither are the Iraqi civilian casualties.

General descriptions of the horrors of war can be read in any military history by John Keegan or Martin Gilbert. But more and more specific accounts of the horrors of war are beginning to see the light of day. *Blood Red Snow: The Memoirs of a German Soldier on the Eastern Front* and *His Time in Hell: A Texas Marine in France* are two recent books that explore the horrors of war from the individual soldier's point of view. Chris Hedges' *What Every Person Should Know About War* is a stinging indictment of the twin evils of the glorification of war and the concealment of its brutality.

Intimate Voices

The recently published *Intimate Voices from the First World War* does all of those things and much more. What makes this book so unique is that the authors—twenty eight men, women, and children from thirteen different nations—because they were not writing for publication, had no particular statement to make other than to describe the effects of war on themselves and their surroundings. This is the ultimate in primary source material. From their research into hundreds of first-hand accounts, the editors of the book, Svetlana Palmer and Sarah Wallis, selected twenty-eight diaries or collections of letters written by soldiers and civilians who lived (and in some cases died) during World War I. Many of the diaries were found decades after the end of the war, and some in the last few years. A few are published here for the first time.

The horrors of war are described here as no historian writing in the twenty-first century could describe them. But in addition to the accounts of death, destruction, and starvation, *Intimate Voices* also gives us an insight into the role of the state in warfare, the religious ideas of the combatants, the war's demoralizing effect on women, and the regrets of soldier and civilian.

The War

The conflict we read about in *Intimate Voices* is the "great war" to "make the world safe for democracy"—the "war to end all wars." The war began when Austria declared war on Serbia after the assassination of Archduke Franz Ferdinand, the heir to the Austro-Hungarian throne, during a state visit to Sarajevo, the capital of the Austro-Hungarian province of Bosnia-Herzegovina. The archduke had recently given an after-dinner toast in which he advocated peace: "To peace! What would we get out of war with Serbia? We'd lose the lives of young men and we'd spend money better used elsewhere. And what would we gain, for heaven's sake? A few plum trees, some pastures full of goat droppings, and a bunch of rebellious killers." His advice went unheeded, and resulted in the slaughter of over a million soldiers who fought for his empire, plus an untold number of ordinary citizens. Overall, 65 million men donned a miliary uniform, over 9.3 million soldiers died, 21 million soldiers were wounded, 7.8 million soldiers were captured or missing, and 6.7 million civilians died.

The Cast of Characters

The writers of the diaries and letters in *Intimate Voices* are a diverse lot.

German soldier Paul Hub is a young recruit sent to make up for the heavy losses suffered by his advancing army. He married his sweetheart, whom he wrote to throughout the war, while home on leave in June of 1918. After a few days with his wife he returned to the front—only to die two months later.

Polish widow Helena Jablonska survived the war and died in 1936.

Austrian doctor Josef Tomann tends to the sick and wounded soldiers in a hospital in Przemysl. He contracted disease and died in May 1915, leaving behind a wife and a baby daughter.

German officer Ernst Nopper, an interior decorator from Ludwigsburg, was killed in action on the Western Front, leaving a wife and two children.

Serbian officer Milorad Markovic is the future grandfather of Mirjana Markovic, wife of Slobodan Milosevic. He survived the war, only to be captured by the Nazis in the next one. He made it through that one as well and died in 1967.

Russian soldier Vasily Mishnin was reunited with his wife and two sons after the war. He went back to work at a furniture shop and died in 1955.

Australian corporal George Mitchell finished the war as a captain. He wrote several books about World War I and served again in World War II. He died in 1961.

Turkish second lieutenant Mehmed Fasih was captured by

the Allies and released at the end of the war. He married in 1924 and lived until 1964.

German doctor Ludwig Deppe returned to Dresden after the war. His subsequent fate is unknown.

French captain Paul Truffrau returned to Paris after the war, where he became a teacher. He went on to fight and keep another diary in World War II. He died in 1973.

Russian officer Dmitry Oskin joined the Bolsheviks after the Russian Revolution. He advanced in the Communist Party but died suddenly in 1934, possibly a victim of a Stalinist purge.

American officer John Clark survived the war and married his sweetheart, a Red Cross nurse.

An unnamed Austrian officer wrote a diary that was found on his dead body in July of 1915. He died in mid-sentence.

Russian soldier Alexei Zyikov was captured by the Germans. His diary was found by a Russian solider in Germany during World War II.

German schoolgirl Piete Kuhr lived through the war and became a professional performer and then a writer. She and her family fled to Switzerland during World War II. She died in 1989.

French schoolboy Yves Congar lived to become a priest, serve in World War II, and be made a cardinal. He lived until 1995.

Klara Hess was the mother of the future Nazi Rudolf Hess.

African Kande Kamara was from French Guinea. He fought for the French and returned home to West Africa at the end of the war. Forced to flee his village, he never saw his family again.

British private Robert Cude returned to London after the war. He later appeared as an extra in a James Bond film.

British officer Richard Meinertzhagen became a colonel and attended the Paris Peace Conference. He became an advocate of Zionism and later wrote *Middle East Diary*, about his experiences in the Middle East after World War I. He died in 1967.

Canadian Winnie McClare was killed in May of 1917, within a month of his arrival at the front line. He was nineteen.

The Horrors of War

There is no better description of the horrors of war than an eyewitness description. German soldier Paul Hub writes to his girlfriend:

I've already seen quite a lot of misery of war. . . . Maria, this sort of a war is so unspeakably miserable. If only you saw a line of stretcher-bearers with their burdens, you'd know what I mean. I haven't had a chance to shoot yet. We're having to deal with an unseen enemy. . . . Every day brings new horrors. . . . Every day the fighting gets fiercer and there is still no end in sight. Our blood is flowing in torrents. . . . That's how it is. All around me, the most gruesome devastation. Dead and wounded soldiers, dead and dying animals, horse cadavers, burnt-out houses, dug-up fields, cars, clothes, weaponry—all this is scattered around me, a real mess. I didn't think war would be like this. We can't sleep for all the noise.

Polish widow Helena Jablonska writes in her diary:

Vast numbers of wounded are being brought in. Many of them die from severe blood loss, but the death toll would not be half as great were it not for cholera. It is spreading so fast that the cases outnumber those wounded and killed in battle. Everything has been infected: carts, stretchers, rooms, wardens, streets, manure, mud, everything. Soldiers fall in battle, where it is impossible to remove the bodies and disinfect them. They don't even bother.

Austrian doctor Josef Tomann writes in his diary:

Starvation is kicking in. Sunken, pale figures wander like corpses through the streets, their ragged clothes hanging from skeletal bodies, their stony faces a picture of utter despair. . . . A terrifying number of people are suffering from malnutrition; the starving arrive in their dozens, frozen soldiers are brought in from the outposts, all of them like walking corpses. They lie silently on their cold hospital beds, make no complaints and drink muddy water they call tea. The next day they are carried away to the morgue. The sight of these pitiful figures, whose wives and children are probably also starving at home, wrings your heart. This is war.

German officer Ernst Nopper writes in his diary:

There are dead bodies everywhere you look. The villages have been completely destroyed. The fields are covered in so many graves it looks like moles have been at work. There are shell holes everywhere.

Serbian officer Milorad Markovic writes in his diary:

I remember things scattered all around; horses and men stumbling and falling into the abyss; Albanian attacks; hosts of women and children. A doctor would not dress an officer's wound; soldiers would not bother to pull out a wounded comrade or officer. Belongings abandoned; starvation; wading across rivers clutching onto horses' tails; old men, women and children climbing up the rocks; dying people on the road; a smashed human skull by the road; a corpse all skin and bones, robbed, stripped naked, mangled; soldiers, police officers, civilians, women, captives. Vlasta's cousin, naked under his overcoat with a collar and cuffs, shattered, gone made. Soldiers like ghosts, skinny, pale, worn out, sunken eyes, their hair and beards long, their clothes in rages, almost naked, barefoot. Ghosts of people begging for bread, walking with sticks, their feet covered in wounds, staggering. Chaos; women in soldiers's clothes; the desperate mothers of those who are too exhausted to go on. A starving soldier who ate too much bread and dropped dead. A soldier selling anything and everything for bread: his gun, clothes, shoes and boots, coats, horses' feedbags, saddlebags, horses.

Russian soldier Vasily Mishnin writes to his pregnant wife:

We go to the depot to get our rifles. Good Lord, what's all

this? They're covered in blood, black clotted lumps of it are hanging off them. . . . It is frightening even to sit or lie down here—the rifle is shaking in my hands. My hand comes down on something black: it turns out there are corpses here that haven't been cleared away. My hair stands on end. I have to sit down. There is no point in staring into the distance—it is pitch dark. All I can feel is fear. I am so frightened of the shells that I want the ground to open up and swallow me. . . . Suddenly a screeching noise pierces the air, I feel a pang in my heart, something whistles past and explodes nearby. My dear Lord, I am so frightened—and I hear this buzzing in my ears. I leave my post and climb into my dugout. It is packed, everyone is shaking and asking again and again, "What's going on? What's going on?" One explosion follows another, and another. Two lads are running, shouting our for nurses. They are covered in blood. It is running down their cheeks and hands, and something else is dripping from underneath their bandages. They're soon dead, shot to pieces. There is screaming, yelling, the earth is shaking from artillery fire and our dugout is rocking from side to side like a boat. . . . Our eyes are full of tears, we wipe them away, but they just keep coming because the shells are full of gas. We are terrified. . . . We will probably never see each other again—all it takes is an instant and I will be no more—and perhaps no one will be able to gather the scattered pieces of my body for burial. . . . A zeppelin attacked Ostrow in the night and dropped a few bombs, many killed. One woman and her two kids got blown to pieces that blew away in the wind.

Australian corporal George Mitchell writes in his diary:

And again I heard the sickening thud of a bullet. I looked at him in horror. The bullet had fearfully mashed his face and gone down his throat, rendering him dumb. But his eyes were dreadful to behold. How he squirmed in agony. There was nothing I could do for him, but pray that he might die swiftly. It took him about twenty minutes to accomplish this and by that time he had tangled his legs in pain and stiffened. I saw the waxy colour creep over his cheek and breathed freer.

Turkish second lieutenant Mehmed Fasih writes in his diary:

> Though I keep picking off lice, there are plenty more—I just can't get rid of them and am itching all over. My body is covered with red and purple blotches. . . . When I finally reach our trenches I find a large pool of blood. It has coagulated and turned black. Bits of brain, bone and flesh are mixed in with it.

German doctor Ludwig Deppe writes in his diary:

> Behind us we have left destroyed fields, ransacked magazines, and, for the immediate future, starvation. We were no longer the agents of culture; our track was marked by death, plundering and evacuated villages.

French captain Paul Truffrau writes in his diary:

> We reach the trench, dug out by joining up the shell-holes and it stinks of bogs and decaying corpses. Stagnant water. . . . The smell of corpses everywhere.

Russian officer Dmitry Oskin writes in his diary:

> The battle became so vicious that our soldiers started using spades to split Austrians' skulls. This hand-to-hand fighting went on for at least two hours. Only nightfall stopped the butchery.

American officer John Clark writes to his sweetheart:

> I was only beginning to see what war really is. . . . Outside of the enemy fire, it was a terrific strain on our men, for we were firing night and day—on a couple of occasions, for ten hours without any intermission. We spent our spare time burying the infantry dead which were scattered all

around us. It was gruesome work, for the bodies had been lying on the battlefield for two, three or more days. On the crest just before us were light "tanks" which had been shattered by German shellfire. They were the most gruesome of all, for the charred bodies of their crews were still in or scattered about them.

The unnamed Austrian officer writes his last words in his diary:

> The wounded groan and cry for their mothers. You have to shut your ears to it. . . . It is enough to drive you insane. Dead, wounded, massive losses. This is the end. Unprecedented slaughter, a horrific bloodbath. There is blood everywhere and the dead and bits of bodies lie scattered about so that

Second only to the horrors on the battlefield are those that one endures in captivity. Russian soldier Alexei Zyikov writes in his diary:

> Hunger does not give you a moment's peace and you are always dreaming of bread: good Russian bread! There is consternation in my soul when I watch people hurling themselves after a piece of bread and a spoonful of soup. We have to work pretty hard too, to the shouts and beatings of the guards, the mocking of the German public. We work from dawn till dusk, sweat mingling with blood; we curse the blows of the rifle butts; I find myself thinking about ending it all, such are the torments of my life in captivity! . . . Then there are those of us who eat potato peel: they take it out of the pit, wash it and boil it, eat it and say how delicious it is. Some consider it the greatest happiness to snatch food from the tub where the Germans throw their leftovers.

War and the State

The truth of Randolph Bourne's classic statement, "War is

the health of the state," can be seen throughout the excerpts from the diaries and letters in *Intimate Voices*. To get a war to work—to get men to kill other men that have never aggressed against them and that they don't even know—the state must do two things: convince men to love the state and to hate the members of other states. The first is always cloaked in patriotism, and leads to an acceptance of interventionism. The second is always cloaked in nationalism, and leads to hatred toward foreigners within one's country. German schoolgirl Piete Kuhr writes in her diary:

> At school they talk of nothing but the war now. The girls are pleased that Germany is entering the field against its old enemy France. We have to learn new songs about the glory of war. The enthusiasm in our town is growing by the hour. . . . People wander through the streets in groups, shouting "Down with Serbia! Long live Germany!" Crowds of people are milling around in the streets, laughing, wishing each other good luck and joining in singing the national anthem. . . . Dear God, just bring the war to an end! I don't look on it as glorious any more, in spite of "school holidays" and victories. . . . At school everyone is so much in favour of the war. . . . They scream so that the headmaster sees what a patriotic school he has. . . . Everyone talks of shortages. Most people are buying in such massive stocks that their cellars are full to bursting. Grandma refuses to do this. She says she doesn't want to deprive the Fatherland of anything. We're not hoarders. The Fatherland won't let us starve. . . . To them [uncle and mother] "the German nation" is still everything. Fall with a cheer for the Fatherland, and you will die as a hero in their eyes.

German officer Ernst Nopper writes in his diary:

> At the border post we strike up "Deutschland, Deutschland Über Alles."

French schoolboy Yves Congar writes in his diary:

I can only think about war. I would like to be a soldier and fight. . . . Very well, if they want to starve us then they'll see when, in the next war, the next generation goes to Germany and starves them. They are turning the French people against them and I'm happy about it. I have never hated them so much. . . . The Germans, fiends, thieves, murderers and arsonists that they are, set fire to everything. . . . The Boches' behaviour in France is scandalous. The loot they are taking back to Germany is unbelievable: they'll have enough to refurbish every one of their towns! But one day soon it will be our turn: we will go there and we will steal, burn and ransack! They had better watch out! Over in Germany they are almost as unhappy as we are. There is famine in all the big cities: Berlin, Dresden and Bavaria; I hope they all die!

Russian soldier Alexei Zyikov writes in his diary:

They boast to us that their governments send them bread and parcels from home. But we, Russians, get nothing: our punishment for fighting badly. Or, perhaps, Mother Russia has forgotten about us.

Klara, the mother of Rudolf Hess, writes to her son:

Of course I know that an armistice would mean your safe return, my sons, but your future and that of the Fatherland would be built on shaky foundations. . . . It would be cowardly of us to worry about you. Instead we should be proud that through our sons we are fighting for the salvation of the Fatherland.

Polish widow Helena Jablonska writes in her diary:

The Jews are frightened. The Russians are taking them in hand now and giving them a taste of the whip. They are being forced to clean the streets and remove manure. . . . The Jewish pogrom has been under way since yesterday evening. The Cossacks waited until the Jews set off to the synagogue for their prayers before setting upon them with whips. They were deaf to any pleas for mercy, regardless of age. . . . It pains me to hear the Germans bad-mouth Galicia. Today I overheard two lieutenants asking "Why on earth should the sons of Germany spill blood to defend this swinish country?" We, the Poles, are hated by everyone in this Austrian hotchpotch and are condemned to serve as prey for all of them.

African Kande Kamara writes in his diary:

We black African soldiers were very sorrowful about the white man's war. There was never any soldier in the camp who knew why we were fighting. There was no time to think about it. I didn't really care who was right—whether it was the French or the Germans—I went to fight with the French army and that was all I knew. The reason for war was never disclosed to any soldier. They didn't tell us how they got into the war. We just fought and fought until we got exhausted and died. Day and night, we fought, killed ourselves, the enemies and everybody else.

Australian corporal George Mitchell writes in his diary:

A wounded Turk told us they regard Australians as fiends incarnate.

British private Robert Cude writes in his diary:

I long to be with battalion so that I can do my best to bereave a German family. I hate these swines. . . . It is a wonderful sight and one that I shall not forget. War such as this, on such a beautiful day seems to me to be quite correct and proper! . . . Men are racing to certain death, and jesting and smiling and cursing, yet wonderfully quiet in a sense, for one feels that one must kill, and as often as one can.

The unnamed Austrian officer writes in his diary:

Since yesterday my mind has been troubled by the thought of the many Austrian heroes who have given their lives

defending the honour of Austria and the Habsburgs, while
I entertained my thoughts of treason, all for the love of an
unworthy [Italian] woman. I am disgusted at myself.
Habsburg, I live for you and I shall die for you, too! . . . He
who gives his life for the Fatherland and the honour of the
Habsburgs shall be honoured and remembered for eternity.

Russian officer Dmitry Oskin writes in his diary of his
support for the ultimate form of state interventionism. First he
records part of a speech he heard given by Lenin in support of
Communism: "The main point is that land should be taken
immediately from the landowners and given to the peasants
without compensation. All ownership of land is to be eliminated." Then he recounts his own comments: "We the sol-
dier-peasants demand that the land be immediately decreed
common property. That it is immediately taken from the
landowners and given to local land committees."

Religion in War

If there is ever a time when men get religious it is certainly
in the midst of a war. The phenomenon of "fox hole religion"
is understandable. What is interesting, however, is the religious
ideas of some combatants when they go into the war. Men on
both sides think that God is on their side. Turkish second
lieutenant Mehmed Fasih writes in his diary:

From the rear comes "Allah! Allah!"—the rallying cry of
our soldiers. . . . One of his comrades tells us how Nuri said
to him when they arrived at the Front together: "I implore
God to let me become a martyr!" Oh Nuri! Your prayer
was answered. We bury Nuri. It was God's will that I would
say the opening verse of the Koran over him.

The African Kande Kamara writes in his diary:

Coming from the background I came from, which was
Muslim oriented, the only thing you thought about was
Allah, death and life. . . . Whatever we thought was dedi-

cated to the God Almighty alone.

This attitude is not restricted to Muslims. The unnamed Austrian officer writes in his diary:

> Dear Lord, come to our aid, for we fight in the name of Justice, the Empire and the Faith. Dear Lord, steer the flight of the double eagle so that these beauteous lands, which had one time belonged to Austria, once again fall under the shadow of its mighty wings. . . . Cases of cholera. This is all we need. Is God no longer on our side? . . . Italy will pay for this, for the Lord sits in judgement up on high and he is wrathful.

German schoolgirl Piete Kuhr writes in her diary:

> But we have faith in France and God, and comfort ourselves with the thought that over in Germany they are almost as unhappy as we are.

Klara, the mother of Rudolf Hess writes to her son:

> Thank God the German Michael [the patron saint of Germany] has finally had the guts to stand firm until our rights to water and land have been secured.

Women in Wartime

One of the great tragedies of war is its demoralizing effect on women, either through subjugation or whoredom. Austrian doctor Josef Tomann writes in his diary:

> And then there are the fat-bellied gents from the commissariat, who stink of fat and go arm in arm with Przemysl's finest ladies, most of who (and this is no exaggeration) have turned into prostitutes of the lowest order. The hospitals have been recruiting teenage girls as nurses, in some places there are up to 50 of them! . . . They are, with very few exceptions, utterly useless. Their main job is to satisfy the

lust of the gentlemen officers and, rather shamefully, of a number of doctors, too. . . . New officers are coming in almost daily with cases of syphilis, gonorrhoea, and soft chancre. Some have all three at once! The poor girls and women feel so flattered when they get chatted up by one of these pestilent pigs in their spotless uniforms, with their shiny boots and buttons. . . . . Anything that can't be carted off or used to pay one of the prostitutes for her services is burnt, so that the Germans don't get it when they march in.

British officer Richard Meinertzhagen writes in his diary:

All the blacks are mad on looting, whether it is the Askaris or the porters, man, woman or child. It is also difficult to stop the blacks from raping women, because they see them as property, like cows or huts.

African Kande Kamara writes in his diary:

The only way to get to town was by sneaking out of camp. There were some white women who had mattresses and beds and invited you to their bedrooms. In fact they tried to keep you there. They gave you clothes, money, and everything. When the inspector came, he never saw you, because you were hiding under the bed or under the bed covers of that beautiful lady. That's how some soldiers got left behind. None of them went back to Africa.

Canadian Winnie McClare writes in a letter to his father:

An awfull lot of fellow that go to London come back in bad shape and are sent to the V.D. hospitals. There is one V.D. hospital near here that has six hundred men in it. It is a shame that the fellows can't keep away from it.

Disillusion and Regret

Occasionally, we read in *Intimate Voices* of the disillusion and regret of soldiers and civilians. The folly of war is sometimes recognized. German officer Ernst Nopper writes in his diary:

> And all this time the weather is so beautiful that the shooting seems absurd.

Russian soldier Vasily Mishnin writes to his pregnant wife:

> What are we suffering for, what do I achieve by killing someone, even a German? . . . It is quite a peaceful scene when it's quiet and no one is firing. This is our enemy? They look like good, normal people, they all want to live and yet here we are, gathered together to take each other's lives away.

British officer Richard Meinertzhagen writes in his diary:

> It seemed so odd that I should be having a meal today with people whom I was trying to kill yesterday. It seemed so wrong and made me wonder whether this really was war or whether we had all made a ghastly mistake.

German officer Ernst Nopper writes in his diary:

> I no longer share most people's enthusiasm for war. I think about the dying soldiers, not just Germans, but also French, English, Russian, Italian, Serbian and I don't know who else.

German schoolgirl Piete Kuhr writes in her diary:

> I don't want any more soldiers to die. Millions are dead— and for what? For whose benefit? We must just make sure that there is never another war in the future. We must never again fall for the nonsense peddled by the older generation.

And finally, the regret of Russian soldier Alexei Zyikov, who writes in his diary during Easter of 1916:

Why did I lead such a debauched life? Why did I not cherish my family and friends? I don't know. I loved adventure and now I am paying for it. I feel very sad. Must I really die like this, fruitlessly, with nothing worth repenting of?

The argument that modern warfare has changed so much that these descriptions of World War I never happen—modern war really isn't all that bad (unless of course you get killed)—is never made by the soldier who suffers psychological damage or psychiatric disorders the rest of his life, the forgotten civilians injured or disfigured in the conflict, or by those maimed or blown up by land mines years later.

Such are the horrors of war.

THE U.S. GLOBAL EMPIRE

There is a new empire in town, and its global presence is increasing every day.

The kingdom of Alexander the Great reached all the way to the borders of India. The Roman Empire controlled the Celtic regions of Northern Europe and all of the Hellenized states that bordered the Mediterranean. The Mongol Empire, which was the largest contiguous empire in history, stretched from Southeast Asia to Europe. The Byzantine Empire spanned the years 395 to 1453. In the sixteenth century, the Ottoman Empire stretched from the Persian Gulf in the east to Hungary in the northwest; and from Egypt in the south to the Caucasus in the north. At the height of its dominion, the British Empire included almost a quarter of the world's population.

Nothing, however, compares to the U.S. global empire. What makes U.S. hegemony unique is that it consists, not of control over great land masses or population centers, but of a global presence unlike that of any other country in history.

The extent of the U.S. global empire is almost incalculable. The latest "Base Structure Report" of the Department of Defense states that the Department's physical assets consist of "more than 600,000 individual buildings and structures, at more than 6,000 locations, on more than 30 million acres." The exact number of locations is then given as 6,702—divided into large installations (115), medium installations (115), and small installations/locations (6,472). This classification can be deceiving, however, because installations are only classified as small if they have a Plant Replacement Value (PRV) of less than $800 million.

Although most of these locations are in the continental United States, 96 of them are in U.S. territories around the globe, and 702 of them are in foreign countries. But as Chalmers Johnson has documented, the figure of 702 foreign military installations is too low, for it does not include installations in Afghanistan, Iraq, Israel, Kosovo, Kuwait, Kyrgyzstan, Qatar, and Uzbekistan. Johnson estimates that an honest count would be closer to 1,000.

The number of countries that the United States has a presence in is staggering. According the U.S. Department of State's list of "Independent States in the World," there are 192 countries in the world, all of which, except Bhutan, Cuba, Iran, and North Korea, have diplomatic relations with the United States. All of these countries except one (Vatican City) are members of the United Nations. According to the Department of Defense publication, "Active Duty Military Personnel Strengths by Regional Area and by Country," the United States has troops in 135 countries. Here is the list:

Afghanistan	Chile
Albania	China
Algeria	Colombia
Antigua	Costa Rica
Argentina	Cote D'lvoire
Australia	Cuba
Austria	Cyprus
Azerbaijan	Czech Republic
Bahamas	Denmark
Bahrain	Djibouti
Bangladesh	Dominican Republic
Barbados	East Timor
Belgium	Ecuador
Belize	Egypt
Bolivia	El Salvador
Bosnia and Herzegovina	Eritrea
Botswana	Estonia
Brazil	Ethiopia
Bulgaria	Fiji
Burma	Finland
Burundi	France
Cambodia	Georgia
Cameroon	Germany
Canada	Ghana
Chad	Greece

Guatemala
Guinea
Haiti
Honduras
Hungary
Iceland
India
Indonesia
Iraq
Ireland
Israel
Italy
Jamaica
Japan
Jordan
Kazakhstan
Kenya
Kuwait
Kyrgyzstan
Laos
Latvia
Lebanon
Liberia
Lithuania
Luxembourg
Macedonia
Madagascar
Malawi
Malaysia
Mali
Malta
Mexico
Mongolia
Morocco
Mozambique
Nepal
Netherlands

New Zealand
Nicaragua
Niger
Nigeria
North Korea
Norway
Oman
Pakistan
Paraguay
Peru
Philippines
Poland
Portugal
Qatar
Republic of the Congo
Romania
Russia
Saudi Arabia
Senegal
Serbia and Montenegro
Sierra Leone
Singapore
Slovenia
Spain
South Africa
South Korea
Sri Lanka
Suriname
Sweden
Switzerland
Syria
Tanzania
Thailand
Togo
Trinidad and Tobago
Tunisia
Turkey

Turkmenistan	Venezuela
Uganda	Vietnam
Ukraine	Yemen
United Arab Emirates	Zambia
United Kingdom	Zimbabwe
Uruguay	

This means that the United States has troops in 70 percent of the world's countries. The average American could probably not locate half of these 135 countries on a map.

To this list could be added regions like the Indian Ocean territory of Diego Garcia, Gibraltar, and the Atlantic Ocean island of St. Helena, all still controlled by Great Britain, but not considered sovereign countries. Greenland is also home to U.S. troops, but is technically part of Denmark. Troops in two other regions, Kosovo and Hong Kong, might also be included here, but the DOD's "Personnel Strengths" document includes U.S. troops in Kosovo under Serbia and U.S. troops in Hong Kong under China.

Possessions of the United States like Guam, Johnston Atoll, Puerto Rico, the Trust Territory of the Pacific Islands, and the Virgin Islands are likewise home to U.S. troops. Guam has over 3,200.

Regular troop strength ranges from a low of 1 in Malawi to a high of 74,796 in Germany. At the time the most recent "Personnel Strengths" was released by the government (September 30, 2003), there were 183,002 troops deployed to Iraq, an unspecified number of which came from U.S. forces in Germany and Italy. The total number of troops deployed abroad as of that date was 252,764, not including U.S. troops in Iraq from the United States. Total military personnel on September 30, 2003, was 1,434,377. This means that 17.6 percent of U.S. military forces were deployed on foreign soil, and certainly over 25 percent if U.S. troops in Iraq from the United States were included. But regardless of how many troops we have in each country, having troops in 135 countries is 135 countries too many.

The U. S. global empire—an empire that Alexander the Great, Caesar Augustus, Genghis Khan, Suleiman the Magnificent, Justinian, and King George V would be proud of.

* * * * *

THE BASES OF EMPIRE

A global empire like the United States needs overseas bases to accommodate its troops, now in 135 countries. Although the latest "Base Structure Report" of the Department of Defense admits to having 96 military installations in U.S. overseas territories and 702 military installations in foreign countries, it has been documented that this number is far too low.

The official list of countries that we have bases in is as follows:

Antigua	Italy
Australia	Japan
Austria	Kenya
Bahamas	Luxembourg
Bahrain	Netherlands
Belgium	New Zealand
Canada	Norway
Colombia	Oman
Cuba	Peru
Denmark	Portugal
Egypt	Singapore
France	Spain
Germany	South Korea
Greece	Turkey
Honduras	United Arab Emirates
Iceland	United Kingdom
Indonesia	Venezuela

To this must be added the bases that we have in Diego Garcia, Greenland, Hong Kong, Kwajalein Atoll, and St. Helena.

This makes a total of 39 foreign locations that the United States officially has bases in, not counting bases in U.S. overseas territories like Guam, Johnston Atoll, Puerto Rico, and the Virgin Islands.

But there are problems with this official list. First of all, it has some notable omissions. The Air Force Technical Applications Center in Thailand is not listed. And neither is Eskan Village and Prince Sultan Air Base in Saudi Arabia. The United States has had a troop presence in the former Soviet Republics of Kyrgyzstan and Uzbekistan since October of 2001, yet they are not listed either. The huge Camp Bondsteel in Kosovo is not even listed, although President Bush has spoken there. According to the Department of Defense publication, "Active Duty Military Personnel Strengths by Regional Area and by Country," the United States has 2,997 active duty military personnel in Qatar. Yet, no base in listed in the Base Structure Report. Incredibly, no bases are even listed in Afghanistan, Kuwait, or Iraq. With critical omissions like these, God only knows how many more foreign bases we have that are not listed.

The issue is not just how many countries the United States has bases in. The issue is U.S. troops on foreign soil. Having an official base just makes our foreign presence worse. It would be better for U.S. troops to patrol our border with Mexico than to patrol the borders of countries half way around the world that most Americans could not locate on a map.

* * * * *

GUARDING THE EMPIRE

When faced with evidence that the U.S. global empire has troops and/or bases in the majority of countries on the planet, apologists for the warfare state and the "military-industrial complex" attempt to dismiss this U.S. global hegemony by claiming that it is the Marine guards at U.S. embassies overseas that account for our presence in so many countries.

It is traditionally believed that the United States has an

embassy in every foreign country and that every foreign country has an embassy in the United States. Most people also think that every U.S. embassy has an attachment of Marine guards to provide security for embassy personnel. Both of these assumptions are wrong.

U.S. Embassies in Foreign Countries

Of the 191 "Independent States in the World" besides the United States, there are 29 countries in which we do not have an embassy:

Andorra	Nauru
Antigua and Barbuda	Palau
Bhutan	Republic of the Congo
Comoros	Saint Kitts and Nevis
Cuba	Saint Lucia
Dominica	Saint Vincent and the Grenadines
Grenada	San Marino
Guinea-Bissau	Sao Tome and Principe
Iran	Seychelles
Kiribati	Solomon Islands
Libya	Somalia
Liechtenstein	Tonga
North Korea	Tuvalu
Maldives	Vanuatu
Monaco	

The United States does not have an embassy in the countries of Bhutan, Cuba, Iran, and North Korea because we do not have diplomatic relations with them.

Many small countries in which the United States has no embassy are "covered" by another country. The U.S. ambassador to Spain is accredited to Andorra. The U.S. ambassador to Barbados is accredited to Antigua and Barbuda, Dominica, Grenada, Saint Kitts and Nevis, Saint Lucia, and Saint Vincent and the Grenadines. The U.S. ambassador to Mauritius is accredited to Seychelles and Comoros. The U.S. ambassador to Senegal is accredited to Guinea-Bissau. The U.S. ambassador to the Marshall Islands is accredited to Kiribati. The U.S. ambassador to Switzerland is accredited to Liechtenstein. The U.S. ambassador to Sri Lanka is accredited to Maldives. The U.S. consul general in Marseille, France, is accredited to Monaco. The U.S. consul general in Florence, Italy, is accredited to San Marino. The U.S. ambassador to Papua New Guinea is accredited to the Solomon Islands and Vanuatu. The U.S. ambassador to Kenya is accredited to Somalia. The U.S. ambassador to Gabon is accredited to Sao Tome and Principe. The U.S. ambassador to Fiji is accredited to Tonga, Tuvalu, and Nauru. The U.S. ambassador to the Philippines is accredited to Palau.

The status of U.S. embassies sometimes changes. In some countries, like Antigua and Barbuda, Guinea-Bissau, Iran, and the Solomon Islands, we used to have an embassy, but it is now closed. The United States has an ambassador to the Republic of the Congo, but the embassy is temporarily collocated with the U.S. embassy in the Democratic Republic of the Congo (formerly called Zaire). The Afghan embassy closed in January 1989 but then reopened in December 2001. In the Central African Republic, the embassy is currently operating with a minimal staff. The United States closed its embassy in Libya in May 1980 and then resumed embassy activities in February 2004 through a U.S. "interest section" in the Belgian embassy. Since June 2004, the United States has maintained a "liaison office" in Libya, but has no immediate plans for an embassy. New embassies had to be built in Kenya and Tanzania after they were bombed in August 1998.

Foreign Embassies in the United States

Just because the United States does not have an embassy in a particular country does not necessarily mean that that country does not have an embassy in the United States. Of the 191 "Independent States in the World" besides the United States, there are 18 countries that do not maintain an embassy in the

United States:

Andorra	Monaco
Bhutan	Nauru
Comoros	San Marino
Cuba	Sao Tome and Principe
Iran	Solomon Islands
Kiribati	Somalia
North Korea	Tonga
Libya	Tuvalu
Maldives	Vanuatu

As mentioned above, the United States does not have diplomatic relations with Bhutan, Cuba, Iran, and North Korea. All of these countries that do not maintain an embassy in Washington D.C. are members of the United Nations and have a representative of some kind at the UN in New York.

There are therefore 11 of these countries that have an embassy in the United States even though we do not have one in their country:

Antigua and Barbuda	Republic of the Congo
Dominica	Saint Kitts and Nevis
Grenada	Saint Lucia
Guinea-Bissau	Saint Vincent and the Grenadines
Liechtenstein	Seychelles
Palau	

There are no countries in which the United States has an embassy that do not likewise have one on U.S. soil.

Marine Security Guards

The question of Marine guards providing security at our embassies is not an easy one to answer. All of our embassies have security measures of some kind, but all are not guarded by U.S. Marines. For security reasons (isn't that always the excuse?), the government does not like to reveal which embassies have Marine guards and which embassies do not.

Marine security guards are members of the Marine Security Guard Battalion headquartered at the Marine Corps base in Quantico, Virginia. Quantico is also the location of the Marine Security Guard School, where guards are trained to react to terrorism, fires, riots, demonstrations, and evacuations.

The stationing of Marine Security Guards at U.S. embassies can be traced to The Foreign Service Act of 1946, which authorizes the Secretary of the Navy, "upon the request of the Secretary of State, to assign enlisted members of the Navy and the Marine Corps to serve as custodians under supervision of the Principal Officer at an Embassy, Legation or Consulate." The first Marine security guards went to Tangier and Bangkok on January 28, 1949. By the end of May 1949, 303 Marines had been assigned to foreign posts. By 1953, this number had increased to 6 officers and 676 enlisted men. By 1956, the number of enlisted men was up to 850.

There are currently over 1,200 Marines serving at over 130 posts abroad, in over 100 countries. Exact figures are not available, but in a report "Concerning the Role of Marine Security Guards in Securing U.S. Embassies and Government Personnel" given before the House Armed Services Committee Special Oversight Panel on Terrorism on October 10, 2002, by W. Ray Williams, the Deputy Assistant Secretary for Counter-measures and Information Security, the number of Marine security guards was given as 1,029 "at 131 US Missions abroad, soon to be 132 with the reactivation of a Marine Security Guard Detachment in Belgrade scheduled for January 2003." He further stated that 19 additional detachments of Marine guards were to be added in the next five years, with a long-term goal of 1,352 Marine guards at 159 detachments. According to the U.S. State Department, as of August 2003, the United States had "over 1,200 Marines for the internal security of 132 U.S. embassies, missions, and consulates worldwide."

Marine security guards are organized into 7 regional companies. Company A headquarters is located in Frankfurt,

Germany, and is responsible for 20 detachments in Eastern Europe. Company B headquarters is located in Nicosia, Cyprus, and is responsible for 18 detachments in northern Africa and the Middle East. Company C headquarters is located in Bangkok, Thailand, and is responsible for 18 detachments located in the Far East, Asia, and Australia. Company D headquarters is located in Ft. Lauderdale, Florida, and is responsible for 26 detachments in Central and South America and the Caribbean. Company E headquarters is also located (with Company A) in Frankfurt, Germany, and is responsible for 16 detachments in Western Europe and Ottawa, Canada. Company F headquarters is located in Nairobi, Kenya, and is responsible for 11 detachments in Sub-Saharan Africa. Company G headquarters is located in Abidjan, Cote d'Ivoire, and is responsible for 12 detachments in West and Central Africa.

Marine security guard companies are commanded by a lieutenant colonel. At each diplomatic post, there is a minimum of one detachment commander and five Marine security guards. This allows them to maintain one security post 24/7. Locations with more than one security post have more than five guards. About 40 percent of detachments have the 1/5 ratio of commander to guards, another 40 percent are between 1/6 and 1/10, and the remaining 20 percent have something greater than 1/10. After graduating from security guard school, a Marine can usually expect two fifteen-month duty tours.

The U.S. Global Empire

What, then, do embassies and Marine guards have to do with the U.S. global empire of troops and bases that garrison the planet? As mentioned at the onset of this article, apologists for the U.S. global empire attempt to dismiss our troop presence in so many countries by claiming that including Marines guarding embassies inflates the total number of countries in which we have a troop presence. The truth, however, is that whether Marine guards are counted or not, the United States still has a global empire that now encompasses 136 countries.

The source for information on U.S. troops stationed abroad is the quarterly publication entitled "Active Duty Military Personnel Strengths by Regional Area and by Country." This is published by a Department of Defense organization called the Directorate for Information Operations and Reports (DIOR). The latest edition that will be referenced in this article is dated March 31, 2004. Previous editions can be seen here. According to the DIOR, the information contained in its report of personnel strengths is provided directly by each branch of the U.S. Armed Forces; that is, the DIOR merely reports the information it receives. The DIOR publication does not indicate why troops are in a particular country, it merely reports the fact that they are there.

The issue here is whether the Marine Corps troops listed as deployed on foreign soil includes Marine guards at embassies. If the figure given for Marines in each country *does not* include embassy guards, then the United States *does* in fact have troops in 136 countries. Case closed. There is no need for this article other than to point out that the United States has added one more country (Guyana) since the first time I addressed the subject of the U.S. global empire. But if the figure given for Marines in each country *does* include embassy guards, then what apologists for the U.S. global empire are saying is that the United States *does not* have troops in 136 countries because Marine guards should not be included. Therefore, so they say, the number of countries in which the U.S. has troops should be limited to those countries in which we actually have bases. Of course, that is a problem as well, but it is not under consideration here since I have previously addressed the subject of the bases of the U.S. empire.

Although the case could be made that these guards are what Lew Rockwell calls "armed servants for the spies and bureaucrats," I am willing to agree with apologists for the U.S. global empire that Marine guards should not be counted when determining whether the United States has troops in other countries. This is also assuming that the "Active Duty Military Personnel Strengths by Regional Area and by Country" document is accurate.

The issue cannot be settled by merely asking the Marine Corps how it determines the number of Marines it has in each country. No one I spoke with in the DOD or the Marine Corps ever heard of the "Active Duty Military Personnel Strengths by Regional Area and by Country" document. And no one in the DOD or the Marine Corps that I sent the document to ever responded. Furthermore, when you start asking questions about Marines guarding U.S. embassies, DOD and Marine Corps officials get nervous (and sometimes downright belligerent) and start asking you questions about why you want the information.

After studying the "Active Duty Military Personnel Strengths by Regional Area and by Country" document, and after determining which countries have a U.S. embassy, it looks as though the figures given for Marines deployed to foreign countries do not include Marine guards at embassies.

Of the 55 countries in which the United States does not have any troops (not just Marines), the following have a U.S. embassy:

Angola	Mauritania
Armenia	Mauritius
Belarus	Micronesia
Benin	Moldova
Brunei	Namibia
Burkina Fasco	Panama
Cape Verde	Papua New Guinea
Central African Republic	Rwanda
Croatia	Samoa
Equatorial Guinea	Slovak Republic
Gabon	Sudan
Gambia	Swaziland
Holy See (The Vatican)	Tajikistan
Lesotho	Uzbekistan
Marshall Islands	

If the figures include Marine guards, then this would mean that no U.S. embassy in any of these 29 countries had Marine security guards.

Some countries in which the United States has Army, Navy, and/or Air Force troops have a U.S. embassy but no Marines are listed as being in the country:

Belize	Malawi
Cambodia	Mongolia
Eritrea	New Zealand
Guyana	Suriname
Lebanon	Ukraine
Madagascar	

If the figures include Marine guards, then this would mean that no U.S. embassy in any of these 11 countries had Marine security guards.

Other countries in which the United States has troops including Marines have a U.S. embassy but do not have the minimum number of 6 Marines necessary for embassy security guard duty.

Albania	Mexico
Botswana	Morocco
Bulgaria	Romania
Cameroon	Serbia and Montenegro
Demo. Republic of the Congo	Sri Lanka
Guinea	Sweden
Iceland	Tanzania
Laos	Zambia
Luxembourg	Zimbabwe
Malaysia	

If the figures include Marine guards, then this would mean that no U.S. embassy in any of these 19 countries had Marine security guards.

There are 13 countries in which the only troops listed are Marines:

Azerbaijan	Mozambique
Burundi	North Korea
Fiji	Sierra Leone
Kyrgyzstan	Trinidad and Tobago
Latvia	Togo
Mali	Turkmenistan
Malta	

The countries of Azerbaijan, Burundi, Fiji, Sierra Leone, and Trinidad and Tobago do not have the minimum number of 6 Marines necessary for embassy security guard duty. If the figures include Marine guards, then this would mean that no U.S. embassy in these 5 countries had Marine security guards. We do not have an embassy in North Korea for Marines to guard. Likewise, there are 167 Marines in Cuba but the United States has no embassy there either.

But supposing that the figure given for Marines in each country does include Marine security guards at embassies, we still have a problem. Most of the countries with a U.S. embassy that have the minimum number of 6 Marines that are necessary to provide embassy security guard duty also have Army, Navy, and/or Air Force troops as well. So whether the figures include Marine guards is irrelevant. The following countries have a U.S. embassy, troops from the Army, Navy, and/or Air Force, and at least 6 Marines:

Afghanistan	Bosnia and Herzegovina
Algeria	Brazil
Argentina	Burma
Australia	Canada
Austria	Chad
Bahamas	Chile
Bahrain	China
Bangladesh	Colombia
Barbados	Costa Rica
Belgium	Cote D'lvoire
Bolivia	Cyprus

Czech Republic	Nepal
Denmark	Netherlands
Djibouti	Nicaragua
Dominican Republic	Niger
Ecuador	Nigeria
Egypt	Norway
El Salvador	Oman
Estonia	Pakistan
Ethiopia	Paraguay
Finland	Peru
France	Philippines
Georgia	Poland
Germany	Portugal
Greece	Qatar
Guatemala	Russia
Guinea	Saudi Arabia
Haiti	Senegal
Honduras	Singapore
Hungary	Slovenia
Iceland	South Africa
India	South Korea
Indonesia/East Timor	Spain
Iraq	Switzerland
Israel	Syria
Italy	Thailand
Jamaica	Tunisia
Japan	Turkey
Jordan	Uganda
Kazakhstan	United Arab Emirates
Kenya	United Kingdom
Kuwait	Uruguay
Liberia	Venezuela
Lithuania	Vietnam
Macedonia	Yemen

The "Personnel Strengths" document includes the country of East Timor under Indonesia so it is impossible to determine exactly how the 10 Marines in that region are divided between the countries.

Of the 13 countries in which the only troops listed are Marines, 6 were previously eliminated because either the United States did not have an embassy in the country or there was not the minimum number of 6 Marines necessary for embassy security guard duty. This leaves only the following seven countries as *potential* examples of countries with a U.S. embassy guarded by Marines that should not be included in the total of 136 countries in which the United States has troops:

Kyrgyzstan	Mozambique
Latvia	Togo
Mali	Turkmenistan
Malta	

But a comparison of the current "Personnel Strengths" document with the previous quarterly editions shows that this is not the case. For example, Kyrgyzstan, which is now listed as having 8 Marines, had 14 Marines three months ago and 27 Marines six months ago. And Malta, which is now listed as having 4 Marines, had 7 Marines three months ago and 3 Marines six months ago. This could not possibly be just Marine embassy guards. The next quarterly report of "Active Duty Military Personnel Strengths by Regional Area and by Country" is sure to have similar changes.

So the fact remains: Marine guards or no Marine guards, the United States has troops in 136 countries.

But even that figure is too low, for the United States also has troops in Dependencies and Areas of Special Sovereignty. These are territories controlled by countries that may be located thousands of miles away from the mother country. For example, the United States has troops in Great Britain and areas controlled by Great Britain such as Gibraltar (on the southern coast of Spain), Diego Garcia (an atoll in the Indian Ocean), and St. Helena (an island in the South Atlantic Ocean). The United States has a 234,022-acre Air Force Base in Greenland, a region controlled by Denmark since 1721. Then there is Kosovo (an autonomous province of Serbia) and Hong Kong (a special administrative region of China).

Aside from the 50 states of the United States, there are also U.S. troops in areas we control like Guam (an island in the Pacific Ocean), Johnston Atoll (an atoll in the Pacific Ocean), Puerto Rico (an island commonwealth in the Caribbean Sea), and the U.S. Virgin Islands (islands between the Caribbean Sea and the North Atlantic Ocean, east of Puerto Rico).

According to the "Personnel Strengths" document, the United States also maintains 23 army personnel in the Trust Territory of the Pacific Islands. After World War II, these island groups in the Pacific Ocean came under the control of the United States. This "Trust Territory" now consists of three sovereign countries (Marshall Islands, Micronesia, and Palau) and the Commonwealth of the Northern Mariana Islands, a commonwealth of the United States.

If these additional areas that have U.S. troops are counted, then it could be said that the United States has troops in 150 countries or territories. It is now easier to list the countries in which the United States does not have troops instead of the other way around. So, although this list could change tomorrow, the following countries are not officially reported as having any U.S. troops:

Andorra	Dominica
Angola	Equatorial Guinea
Armenia	Gabon
Belarus	Gambia
Benin	Grenada
Bhutan	Guinea-Bissau
Brunei	Holy See (The Vatican)
Burkina Faso	Iran
Cape Verde	Kiribati
Central African Republic	Lesotho
Comoros	Libya
Croatia	Liechtenstein

Maldives	Samoa
Mauritania	San Marino
Mauritius	Sao Tome and Principe
Moldova	Seychelles
Monaco	Slovak Republic
Namibia	Solomon Islands
Nauru	Somalia
Panama	Sudan
Papua New Guinea	Swaziland
Republic of the Congo	Tajikistan
Rwanda	Tonga
Saint Kitts and Nevis	Tuvalu
Saint Lucia	Uzbekistan
Saint Vincent and the Grenadines	Vanuatu

U.S. Foreign Policy

In his Farewell Address, George Washington warned against "permanent alliances with any portion of the foreign world" and said that the United States should have "as little political connection as possible" with foreign nations. But he also warned us about "those overgrown military establishments which, under any form of government, are inauspicious to liberty, and which are to be regarded as particularly hostile to republican liberty."

If any country ever had an overgrown military establishment, it is the United States and its military juggernaut. Before the recent Iraq war, the United States outspent the "evil" rogue nations of Iraq, Syria, Iran, North Korea, Libya, and Cuba on defense spending by a ratio of twenty-two to one. The actual amount that the United States spent on "defense" during fiscal year 2004 has been estimated by Robert Higgs to be about $695 billion. The United States is also the biggest arms exporter, accounting for about half of all global arms exports.

Most of this spending could be eliminated if the United States returned to the foreign policy ideas of the Founders. Current U.S. foreign policy can only be described as reckless, interventionist, militaristic, and belligerent. This can lead to severe consequences, as Chalmers Johnson has pointed out in his incredible book *Blowback: The Costs and Consequences of American Empire*, "The suicidal assassins of September 11, 2001, did not 'attack America,' as political leaders and news media in the United States have tried to maintain; they attacked American foreign policy."

The U.S. Empire is greatly overextended. Buried on page 362 of the 9/11 Commission Report is an admission that the entire planet is our manifest destiny:

> Now threats can emerge quickly. An organization like al Qaeda, headquartered in a country on the other side of the earth, in a region so poor that electricity or telephones were scarce, could nonetheless scheme to wield weapons of unprecedented destructive power in the largest cities of the United States. In this sense, 9/11 has taught us that terrorism against American interests "over there" should be regarded just as we regard terrorism against America "over here." In this same sense, the American homeland is the planet.

The 9/11 attacks were just the beginning of a worldwide revolt against the current U.S. foreign policy of a global empire. Only a Jeffersonian foreign policy of peace, commerce, friendship, and no entangling alliances can arrest the menacing U.S. Empire.

* * * * *

FOR FURTHER READING

Amans, Veritatis, et al. *Christianity and War*. Pensacola: Classic Reprints, 2003.

Blum, William. *Rogue State: A Guide to the World's Only Superpower*. Monroe: Common Courage Press, 2000.

Bovard, James. *Terrorism and Tyranny*. New York: Palgrave Macmillan, 2003.

_____. *The Bush Betrayal*. New York: Palgrave Macmillan, 2004.

Buchanan, Patrick J. *A Republic, Not an Empire: Reclaiming America's Destiny*. Washington D.C.: Regnery Publishing, 1999.

_____. *Where the Right Went Wrong: How Neoconservatives Subverted the Reagan Revolution and Hijacked the Bush Presidency*. New York: Thomas Dunne Books, 2004.

Butler, Smedley D., and Adam Parfrey. *War Is a Racket: The Anti-War Classic by America's Most Decorated General, Two Other Anti-Interventionist Tracts, and Photographs from the Horror of It*. Los Angeles: Feral House, 2003.

Carroll, James. *Crusade: Chronicles of an Unjust War*. New York: Metropolitan Books, 2004.

Chomsky, Noam. *Hegemony or Survival: America's Quest for Global Dominance*. New York: Metropolitan Books, 2003.

Denson, John V. *The Costs of War: America's Pyrrhic Victories*, 2nd expanded ed. New Brunswick: Transaction Publishers, 1999.

Ebeling, Richard M., and Jacob G. Hornberger, eds. *The Failure of America's Foreign Wars*. Fairfax: The Future of Freedom Foundation, 1996.

Fleming, Thomas J. *The Illusion of Victory: America in World War I*. New York: Basic Books, 2003.

Hedges, Chris. *War is a Force that Gives Us Meaning*. New

York: Public Affairs, 2002.

_____. *What Every Person Should Know About War*. New York: Free Press, 2003.

Higgs, Robert, ed. *Arms, Politics, and the Economy: Historical and Contemporary Perspectives*. New York: Holmes & Meier Publishers, 1990.

Hoppe, Hans-Hermann, ed., *The Myth of National Defense*. Auburn: Ludwig von Mises Institute, 2003.

Johnson, Chalmers. *Blowback: The Costs and Consequences of American Empire*. New York: Owl Books, 2004.

_____. *The Sorrows of Empire: Military, Secrecy, and the End of the Republic*. New York: Metropolitan Books, 2004.

Kolko, Gabriel. *Another Century of War?* New York: The New Press, 2002.

_____. *Century of War: Politics, Conflicts, and Society Since 1914*. New York: The New Press, 1994.

Opitz, Edmund A., ed. *Leviathan at War*. Irvington-on-Hudson: Foundation for Economic Education, 1995.

Palmer, Svetlana, and Sarah Wallis, eds. *Intimate Voices from the First World War*. New York: William Morrow, 2003.

Porter, Bruce D. *War and the Rise of the State: The Military Foundations of Modern Politics*. New York: The Free Press, 1994.

Quigley, John B. *The Ruses for War: American Interventionism Since World War II*. Buffalo: Prometheus Books, 1992.

Ryn, Claes. *America the Virtuous: The Crisis of Democracy and the Quest for Empire*. New Brunswick: Transaction Publishers, 2003.

Schaffer, Ronald. *America in the Great War: The Rise of the War Welfare State*. New York: Oxford University Press, 1991.

Stromberg, Joseph R. *War, Peace, and the State*. An Annotated War Bibliography. http://www.lewrockwell.com/stromberg/stromberg23.html.

Yoder, John Howard. *When War is Unjust: Being Honest in Just-War Thinking*, 2nd ed. Eugene: Wipf and Stock Publishers, 2001.